C-4994   CAREER EXAMINATION SERIES

This is your
PASSBOOK for...

CWEA Mechanical Technologist

Test Preparation Study Guide
Questions & Answers

NLC® NATIONAL LEARNING CORPORATION®

COPYRIGHT NOTICE

This book is SOLELY intended for, is sold ONLY to, and its use is RESTRICTED to individual, bona fide applicants or candidates who qualify by virtue of having seriously filed applications for appropriate license, certificate, professional and/or promotional advancement, higher school matriculation, scholarship, or other legitimate requirements of education and/or governmental authorities.

This book is NOT intended for use, class instruction, tutoring, training, duplication, copying, reprinting, excerption, or adaptation, etc., by:

1) Other publishers
2) Proprietors and/or Instructors of "Coaching" and/or Preparatory Courses
3) Personnel and/or Training Divisions of commercial, industrial, and governmental organizations
4) Schools, colleges, or universities and/or their departments and staffs, including teachers and other personnel
5) Testing Agencies or Bureaus
6) Study groups which seek by the purchase of a single volume to copy and/or duplicate and/or adapt this material for use by the group as a whole without having purchased individual volumes for each of the members of the group
7) Et al.

Such persons would be in violation of appropriate Federal and State statutes.

PROVISION OF LICENSING AGREEMENTS – Recognized educational, commercial, industrial, and governmental institutions and organizations, and others legitimately engaged in educational pursuits, including training, testing, and measurement activities, may address request for a licensing agreement to the copyright owners, who will determine whether, and under what conditions, including fees and charges, the materials in this book may be used them. In other words, a licensing facility exists for the legitimate use of the material in this book on other than an individual basis. However, it is asseverated and affirmed here that the material in this book CANNOT be used without the receipt of the express permission of such a licensing agreement from the Publishers. Inquiries re licensing should be addressed to the company, attention rights and permissions department.

All rights reserved, including the right of reproduction in whole or in part, in any form or by any means, electronic or mechanical, including photocopying, recording, or by any information storage and retrieval system, without permission in writing from the Publisher.

Copyright © 2024 by
National Learning Corporation

212 Michael Drive, Syosset, NY 11791
(516) 921-8888 • www.passbooks.com
E-mail: info@passbooks.com

PUBLISHED IN THE UNITED STATES OF AMERICA

PASSBOOK® SERIES

THE *PASSBOOK® SERIES* has been created to prepare applicants and candidates for the ultimate academic battlefield – the examination room.

At some time in our lives, each and every one of us may be required to take an examination – for validation, matriculation, admission, qualification, registration, certification, or licensure.

Based on the assumption that every applicant or candidate has met the basic formal educational standards, has taken the required number of courses, and read the necessary texts, the *PASSBOOK® SERIES* furnishes the one special preparation which may assure passing with confidence, instead of failing with insecurity. Examination questions – together with answers – are furnished as the basic vehicle for study so that the mysteries of the examination and its compounding difficulties may be eliminated or diminished by a sure method.

This book is meant to help you pass your examination provided that you qualify and are serious in your objective.

The entire field is reviewed through the huge store of content information which is succinctly presented through a provocative and challenging approach – the question-and-answer method.

A climate of success is established by furnishing the correct answers at the end of each test.

You soon learn to recognize types of questions, forms of questions, and patterns of questioning. You may even begin to anticipate expected outcomes.

You perceive that many questions are repeated or adapted so that you can gain acute insights, which may enable you to score many sure points.

You learn how to confront new questions, or types of questions, and to attack them confidently and work out the correct answers.

You note objectives and emphases, and recognize pitfalls and dangers, so that you may make positive educational adjustments.

Moreover, you are kept fully informed in relation to new concepts, methods, practices, and directions in the field.

You discover that you are actually taking the examination all the time: you are preparing for the examination by "taking" an examination, not by reading extraneous and/or supererogatory textbooks.

In short, this PASSBOOK®, used directedly, should be an important factor in helping you to pass your test.

CWEA MECHANICAL TECHNOLOGIST

EXAM CONTENT

CWEA's Technical Certification Program Mechanical Technologist exams are based on exam blueprints that outline the exam content and are periodically reviewed by CWEA Subject Matter Experts. An exam blueprint is based on a job task analysis that includes research of the essential duties of a Mechanical Technologist worker at a representative cross-section of systems and facilities.

The exam content outline that follows presents content covered on the Mechanical Technologist exams and shows the amount of the exam devoted to each Domain in the column labeled weighting.

MT GRADE 1 EXAM CONTENT OUTLINE

Content Domain	Weighting
Domain 1 – Inspection, Maintenance, Installation and Repair	28%
Domain 2 – Tools and Equipment	20%
Domain 3 – Records, Reports and SCADA	10%
Domain 4 – Safety and Facility Maintenance	22%
Domain 5 – Communication	9%
Domain 6 – Math	11%
TOTAL	100%

Domain 1 – Inspection, Maintenance, Installation and Repair

Sub-Domain 1.1:
Inspection of systems and equipment
1. Assist in the general inspection of water/wastewater plant and/or lift/pump station mechanical components (pumps, valves, motors, engines, compressors, actuators, computerized pneumatic and odor control systems, etc.)
2. Assist in identifying and troubleshooting mechanical problems
3. Assist in the tuning of engines, adjusting and setting valve clearance, cleaning and adjusting regulators, cleaning and inspecting magnetic points, cleaning and adjusting engine timing, and checking fueling and other controls and devices
4. Inspect small motorized equipment and vehicles

Sub-Domain 1.2:
Maintenance and repair of tools, equipment, systems and facilities
1. Assist in the disassembly and reassembly of equipment in order to clean parts and cases
2. Perform general clean-up of tools, equipment and work areas

3. Assist in the maintenance and repair of equipment used for disinfection of water/wastewater treatment facilities, including the connection and disconnection of cylinders
4. Clean, oil and lubricate motors, generators, compressors, pumps, turbines and other moving equipment
5. Assist in the inspection, calibration and maintenance of equipment used for confined space entries (atmospheric monitors, air testers, etc.)
6. Assist with regularly scheduled preventative maintenance and repair work on water/wastewater plant and lift/pump station equipment, pipelines and valves
7. Assist in the maintenance of mechanical equipment necessary to the operation of water/wastewater facilities, including large pumps, portable gas and diesel-driven pumps, motors, hydraulic controls and regulators, valves and allied pumping systems, chemical feed and processing equipment, compressors, heating and ventilating equipment, emergency generators, and all other related equipment

Sub-Domain 1.3:
Installation of components and equipment
1. Assist in the installation of plant, field and shop equipment, components and machinery

Domain 2 – Tools and Equipment

Sub-Domain 2.1:
Design and fabrication of equipment
1. Assist in the fabrication and assembly of a variety of equipment and specialty tools
2. Assist in the fabrication of parts and fittings, making of assemblies, and repair of units based on drawings, specifications, sketches, work orders, verbal instructions or personal visual inspection

Sub-Domain 2.2:
Meters
1. Read and interpret meters accurately
2. Chart and record results
3. Notify senior staff members of issues

Sub-Domain 2.3:
Operation of tools, equipment and vehicles
1. Assist in the operation of a crane or rigging equipment for moving/placing pumps, machinery or other heavy equipment during installation, maintenance and repair activities
2. Operate vehicles used for installation, maintenance and repair activities (trucks, forklifts, vactors)
3. Operate equipment used for installation, maintenance and repair activities (portable and stationary generators, steam cleaners, portable pumps, compressors, valves, pumps, gauges, engines and electromechanical devices)

4. Operate hand and power tools used for installation, maintenance and repair activities (sandblaster, grinder, pneumatic, hydraulic and electric tools, oxygen-acetylene torch)
5. Operate precision measuring instruments in the performance of various work assignments (calipers, micrometers, dial indicators)

Domain 3 – Records, Reports and SCADA

Sub-Domain 3.1:
Documentation
1. Basic understanding of the importance of accurate documentation
2. Assist in the preparation of work orders and field reports
3. Record date and run times for pump motors, standby generators and related equipment
4. Basic understanding of workflow process and documentation in computerized maintenance management system (CMMS)
5. Follow Operations and Maintenance Manual (OMM) and standard operating procedures (SOPs)

Sub-Domain 3.2:
Supervisory Control and Data Acquisition (SCADA)
1. Basic understanding of Supervisory Control and Data Acquisition (SCADA) system
2. Assist in identifying the status of a station or plant based on SCADA information

Domain 4 – Safety and Facility Maintenance

Sub-Domain 4.1:
Safety
1. Knowledge of basic safety rules and safe work practices
2. Basic knowledge of CalOSHA standards and safety procedures for working with chemicals (e.g. Safety Data Sheets)
3. Basic knowledge of safety practices for confined space entry
4. Assist with confined space entries per CalOSHA and local regulations
5. Perform vehicle, tool and equipment safety checks and air-quality tests
6. Follow Lockout Tagout (LOTO) safety procedures
7. Identify and implement proper Personal Protective Equipment (PPE) for work environment (safety glasses, hard hat, gloves, ear protection, respirator, face shield, hazmat suit)

Sub-Domain 4.2:
Building and grounds maintenance
1. Assist with building and grounds maintenance including plumbing, painting, moving furniture, basic carpentry, masonry and irrigation
2. Perform housekeeping duties in facilities including cleaning and removing waste products, cleaning screens and vents, and performing janitorial tasks

3. Basic knowledge of general methods of related electrical, carpentry, plumbing, HVAC and pipefitting repair to identify building and grounds maintenance and repair issues

Domain 5 – Communication

Sub-Domain 5.1:
Communication
1. Communicate clearly and concisely, both orally and in writing
2. Understand and follow oral and written instructions
3. Establish and maintain cooperative working relationships with those contacted in the course of work, including peers, operators, superiors, vendors, contractors, customers and the general public

Domain 6 – Math

Sub-Domain 6.1:
Math calculations and basic computations
1. Calculate flow rates
2. Calculate volume and area
3. Calculate pressure
4. Basic understanding of converting metric and American standard measurements

HOW TO TAKE A TEST

I. YOU MUST PASS AN EXAMINATION

A. WHAT EVERY CANDIDATE SHOULD KNOW

Examination applicants often ask us for help in preparing for the written test. What can I study in advance? What kinds of questions will be asked? How will the test be given? How will the papers be graded?

As an applicant for a civil service examination, you may be wondering about some of these things. Our purpose here is to suggest effective methods of advance study and to describe civil service examinations.

Your chances for success on this examination can be increased if you know how to prepare. Those "pre-examination jitters" can be reduced if you know what to expect. You can even experience an adventure in good citizenship if you know why civil service exams are given.

B. WHY ARE CIVIL SERVICE EXAMINATIONS GIVEN?

Civil service examinations are important to you in two ways. As a citizen, you want public jobs filled by employees who know how to do their work. As a job seeker, you want a fair chance to compete for that job on an equal footing with other candidates. The best-known means of accomplishing this two-fold goal is the competitive examination.

Exams are widely publicized throughout the nation. They may be administered for jobs in federal, state, city, municipal, town or village governments or agencies.

Any citizen may apply, with some limitations, such as the age or residence of applicants. Your experience and education may be reviewed to see whether you meet the requirements for the particular examination. When these requirements exist, they are reasonable and applied consistently to all applicants. Thus, a competitive examination may cause you some uneasiness now, but it is your privilege and safeguard.

C. HOW ARE CIVIL SERVICE EXAMS DEVELOPED?

Examinations are carefully written by trained technicians who are specialists in the field known as "psychological measurement," in consultation with recognized authorities in the field of work that the test will cover. These experts recommend the subject matter areas or skills to be tested; only those knowledges or skills important to your success on the job are included. The most reliable books and source materials available are used as references. Together, the experts and technicians judge the difficulty level of the questions.

Test technicians know how to phrase questions so that the problem is clearly stated. Their ethics do not permit "trick" or "catch" questions. Questions may have been tried out on sample groups, or subjected to statistical analysis, to determine their usefulness.

Written tests are often used in combination with performance tests, ratings of training and experience, and oral interviews. All of these measures combine to form the best-known means of finding the right person for the right job.

II. HOW TO PASS THE WRITTEN TEST

A. NATURE OF THE EXAMINATION

To prepare intelligently for civil service examinations, you should know how they differ from school examinations you have taken. In school you were assigned certain definite pages to read or subjects to cover. The examination questions were quite detailed and usually emphasized memory. Civil service exams, on the other hand, try to discover your present ability to perform the duties of a position, plus your potentiality to learn these duties. In other words, a civil service exam attempts to predict how successful you will be. Questions cover such a broad area that they cannot be as minute and detailed as school exam questions.

In the public service similar kinds of work, or positions, are grouped together in one "class." This process is known as *position-classification*. All the positions in a class are paid according to the salary range for that class. One class title covers all of these positions, and they are all tested by the same examination.

B. FOUR BASIC STEPS

1) Study the announcement

How, then, can you know what subjects to study? Our best answer is: "Learn as much as possible about the class of positions for which you've applied." The exam will test the knowledge, skills and abilities needed to do the work.

Your most valuable source of information about the position you want is the official exam announcement. This announcement lists the training and experience qualifications. Check these standards and apply only if you come reasonably close to meeting them.

The brief description of the position in the examination announcement offers some clues to the subjects which will be tested. Think about the job itself. Review the duties in your mind. Can you perform them, or are there some in which you are rusty? Fill in the blank spots in your preparation.

Many jurisdictions preview the written test in the exam announcement by including a section called "Knowledge and Abilities Required," "Scope of the Examination," or some similar heading. Here you will find out specifically what fields will be tested.

2) Review your own background

Once you learn in general what the position is all about, and what you need to know to do the work, ask yourself which subjects you already know fairly well and which need improvement. You may wonder whether to concentrate on improving your strong areas or on building some background in your fields of weakness. When the announcement has specified "some knowledge" or "considerable knowledge," or has used adjectives like "beginning principles of..." or "advanced ... methods," you can get a clue as to the number and difficulty of questions to be asked in any given field. More questions, and hence broader coverage, would be included for those subjects which are more important in the work. Now weigh your strengths and weaknesses against the job requirements and prepare accordingly.

3) Determine the level of the position

Another way to tell how intensively you should prepare is to understand the level of the job for which you are applying. Is it the entering level? In other words, is this the position in which beginners in a field of work are hired? Or is it an intermediate or advanced level? Sometimes this is indicated by such words as "Junior" or "Senior" in the class title. Other jurisdictions use Roman numerals to designate the level – Clerk I, Clerk II, for example. The word "Supervisor" sometimes appears in the title. If the level is not indicated by the title, check the description of duties. Will you be working under very close supervision, or will you have responsibility for independent decisions in this work?

4) Choose appropriate study materials

Now that you know the subjects to be examined and the relative amount of each subject to be covered, you can choose suitable study materials. For beginning level jobs, or even advanced ones, if you have a pronounced weakness in some aspect of your training, read a modern, standard textbook in that field. Be sure it is up to date and has general coverage. Such books are normally available at your library, and the librarian will be glad to help you locate one. For entry-level positions, questions of appropriate difficulty are chosen -- neither highly advanced questions, nor those too simple. Such questions require careful thought but not advanced training.

If the position for which you are applying is technical or advanced, you will read more advanced, specialized material. If you are already familiar with the basic principles of your field, elementary textbooks would waste your time. Concentrate on advanced textbooks and technical periodicals. Think through the concepts and review difficult problems in your field.

These are all general sources. You can get more ideas on your own initiative, following these leads. For example, training manuals and publications of the government agency which employs workers in your field can be useful, particularly for technical and professional positions. A letter or visit to the government department involved may result in more specific study suggestions, and certainly will provide you with a more definite idea of the exact nature of the position you are seeking.

III. KINDS OF TESTS

Tests are used for purposes other than measuring knowledge and ability to perform specified duties. For some positions, it is equally important to test ability to make adjustments to new situations or to profit from training. In others, basic mental abilities not dependent on information are essential. Questions which test these things may not appear as pertinent to the duties of the position as those which test for knowledge and information. Yet they are often highly important parts of a fair examination. For very general questions, it is almost impossible to help you direct your study efforts. What we can do is to point out some of the more common of these general abilities needed in public service positions and describe some typical questions.

1) General information

Broad, general information has been found useful for predicting job success in some kinds of work. This is tested in a variety of ways, from vocabulary lists to questions about current events. Basic background in some field of work, such as sociology or economics, may be sampled in a group of questions. Often these are principles which have become familiar to most persons through exposure rather than through formal training. It is difficult to advise you how to study for these questions; being alert to the world around you is our best suggestion.

2) Verbal ability

An example of an ability needed in many positions is verbal or language ability. Verbal ability is, in brief, the ability to use and understand words. Vocabulary and grammar tests are typical measures of this ability. Reading comprehension or paragraph interpretation questions are common in many kinds of civil service tests. You are given a paragraph of written material and asked to find its central meaning.

3) Numerical ability

Number skills can be tested by the familiar arithmetic problem, by checking paired lists of numbers to see which are alike and which are different, or by interpreting charts and graphs. In the latter test, a graph may be printed in the test booklet which you are asked to use as the basis for answering questions.

4) Observation

A popular test for law-enforcement positions is the observation test. A picture is shown to you for several minutes, then taken away. Questions about the picture test your ability to observe both details and larger elements.

5) Following directions

In many positions in the public service, the employee must be able to carry out written instructions dependably and accurately. You may be given a chart with several columns, each column listing a variety of information. The questions require you to carry out directions involving the information given in the chart.

6) Skills and aptitudes

Performance tests effectively measure some manual skills and aptitudes. When the skill is one in which you are trained, such as typing or shorthand, you can practice. These tests are often very much like those given in business school or high school courses. For many of the other skills and aptitudes, however, no short-time preparation can be made. Skills and abilities natural to you or that you have developed throughout your lifetime are being tested.

Many of the general questions just described provide all the data needed to answer the questions and ask you to use your reasoning ability to find the answers. Your best preparation for these tests, as well as for tests of facts and ideas, is to be at your physical and mental best. You, no doubt, have your own methods of getting into an exam-taking mood and keeping "in shape." The next section lists some ideas on this subject.

IV. KINDS OF QUESTIONS

Only rarely is the "essay" question, which you answer in narrative form, used in civil service tests. Civil service tests are usually of the short-answer type. Full instructions for answering these questions will be given to you at the examination. But in case this is your first experience with short-answer questions and separate answer sheets, here is what you need to know:

1) Multiple-choice Questions

Most popular of the short-answer questions is the "multiple choice" or "best answer" question. It can be used, for example, to test for factual knowledge, ability to solve problems or judgment in meeting situations found at work.

A multiple-choice question is normally one of three types—
- It can begin with an incomplete statement followed by several possible endings. You are to find the one ending which *best* completes the statement, although some of the others may not be entirely wrong.
- It can also be a complete statement in the form of a question which is answered by choosing one of the statements listed.

- It can be in the form of a problem – again you select the best answer.

Here is an example of a multiple-choice question with a discussion which should give you some clues as to the method for choosing the right answer:

When an employee has a complaint about his assignment, the action which will *best* help him overcome his difficulty is to
- A. discuss his difficulty with his coworkers
- B. take the problem to the head of the organization
- C. take the problem to the person who gave him the assignment
- D. say nothing to anyone about his complaint

In answering this question, you should study each of the choices to find which is best. Consider choice "A" – Certainly an employee may discuss his complaint with fellow employees, but no change or improvement can result, and the complaint remains unresolved. Choice "B" is a poor choice since the head of the organization probably does not know what assignment you have been given, and taking your problem to him is known as "going over the head" of the supervisor. The supervisor, or person who made the assignment, is the person who can clarify it or correct any injustice. Choice "C" is, therefore, correct. To say nothing, as in choice "D," is unwise. Supervisors have and interest in knowing the problems employees are facing, and the employee is seeking a solution to his problem.

2) True/False Questions

The "true/false" or "right/wrong" form of question is sometimes used. Here a complete statement is given. Your job is to decide whether the statement is right or wrong.

SAMPLE: A roaming cell-phone call to a nearby city costs less than a non-roaming call to a distant city.

This statement is wrong, or false, since roaming calls are more expensive.

This is not a complete list of all possible question forms, although most of the others are variations of these common types. You will always get complete directions for answering questions. Be sure you understand *how* to mark your answers – ask questions until you do.

V. RECORDING YOUR ANSWERS

Computer terminals are used more and more today for many different kinds of exams.

For an examination with very few applicants, you may be told to record your answers in the test booklet itself. Separate answer sheets are much more common. If this separate answer sheet is to be scored by machine – and this is often the case – it is highly important that you mark your answers correctly in order to get credit.

An electronic scoring machine is often used in civil service offices because of the speed with which papers can be scored. Machine-scored answer sheets must be marked with a pencil, which will be given to you. This pencil has a high graphite content which responds to the electronic scoring machine. As a matter of fact, stray dots may register as answers, so do not let your pencil rest on the answer sheet while you are pondering the correct answer. Also, if your pencil lead breaks or is otherwise defective, ask for another.

Since the answer sheet will be dropped in a slot in the scoring machine, be careful not to bend the corners or get the paper crumpled.

The answer sheet normally has five vertical columns of numbers, with 30 numbers to a column. These numbers correspond to the question numbers in your test booklet. After each number, going across the page are four or five pairs of dotted lines. These short dotted lines have small letters or numbers above them. The first two pairs may also have a "T" or "F" above the letters. This indicates that the first two pairs only are to be used if the questions are of the true-false type. If the questions are multiple choice, disregard the "T" and "F" and pay attention only to the small letters or numbers.

Answer your questions in the manner of the sample that follows:

32. The largest city in the United States is
    A. Washington, D.C.
    B. New York City
    C. Chicago
    D. Detroit
    E. San Francisco

1) Choose the answer you think is best. (New York City is the largest, so "B" is correct.)
2) Find the row of dotted lines numbered the same as the question you are answering. (Find row number 32)
3) Find the pair of dotted lines corresponding to the answer. (Find the pair of lines under the mark "B.")
4) Make a solid black mark between the dotted lines.

VI. BEFORE THE TEST

Common sense will help you find procedures to follow to get ready for an examination. Too many of us, however, overlook these sensible measures. Indeed, nervousness and fatigue have been found to be the most serious reasons why applicants fail to do their best on civil service tests. Here is a list of reminders:

- Begin your preparation early – Don't wait until the last minute to go scurrying around for books and materials or to find out what the position is all about.
- Prepare continuously – An hour a night for a week is better than an all-night cram session. This has been definitely established. What is more, a night a week for a month will return better dividends than crowding your study into a shorter period of time.
- Locate the place of the exam – You have been sent a notice telling you when and where to report for the examination. If the location is in a different town or otherwise unfamiliar to you, it would be well to inquire the best route and learn something about the building.
- Relax the night before the test – Allow your mind to rest. Do not study at all that night. Plan some mild recreation or diversion; then go to bed early and get a good night's sleep.
- Get up early enough to make a leisurely trip to the place for the test – This way unforeseen events, traffic snarls, unfamiliar buildings, etc. will not upset you.
- Dress comfortably – A written test is not a fashion show. You will be known by number and not by name, so wear something comfortable.

- Leave excess paraphernalia at home – Shopping bags and odd bundles will get in your way. You need bring only the items mentioned in the official notice you received; usually everything you need is provided. Do not bring reference books to the exam. They will only confuse those last minutes and be taken away from you when in the test room.
- Arrive somewhat ahead of time – If because of transportation schedules you must get there very early, bring a newspaper or magazine to take your mind off yourself while waiting.
- Locate the examination room – When you have found the proper room, you will be directed to the seat or part of the room where you will sit. Sometimes you are given a sheet of instructions to read while you are waiting. Do not fill out any forms until you are told to do so; just read them and be prepared.
- Relax and prepare to listen to the instructions
- If you have any physical problem that may keep you from doing your best, be sure to tell the test administrator. If you are sick or in poor health, you really cannot do your best on the exam. You can come back and take the test some other time.

VII. AT THE TEST

The day of the test is here and you have the test booklet in your hand. The temptation to get going is very strong. Caution! There is more to success than knowing the right answers. You must know how to identify your papers and understand variations in the type of short-answer question used in this particular examination. Follow these suggestions for maximum results from your efforts:

1) Cooperate with the monitor

The test administrator has a duty to create a situation in which you can be as much at ease as possible. He will give instructions, tell you when to begin, check to see that you are marking your answer sheet correctly, and so on. He is not there to guard you, although he will see that your competitors do not take unfair advantage. He wants to help you do your best.

2) Listen to all instructions

Don't jump the gun! Wait until you understand all directions. In most civil service tests you get more time than you need to answer the questions. So don't be in a hurry. Read each word of instructions until you clearly understand the meaning. Study the examples, listen to all announcements and follow directions. Ask questions if you do not understand what to do.

3) Identify your papers

Civil service exams are usually identified by number only. You will be assigned a number; you must not put your name on your test papers. Be sure to copy your number correctly. Since more than one exam may be given, copy your exact examination title.

4) Plan your time

Unless you are told that a test is a "speed" or "rate of work" test, speed itself is usually not important. Time enough to answer all the questions will be provided, but this does not mean that you have all day. An overall time limit has been set. Divide the total time (in minutes) by the number of questions to determine the approximate time you have for each question.

5) Do not linger over difficult questions

If you come across a difficult question, mark it with a paper clip (useful to have along) and come back to it when you have been through the booklet. One caution if you do this – be sure to skip a number on your answer sheet as well. Check often to be sure that you have not lost your place and that you are marking in the row numbered the same as the question you are answering.

6) Read the questions

Be sure you know what the question asks! Many capable people are unsuccessful because they failed to *read* the questions correctly.

7) Answer all questions

Unless you have been instructed that a penalty will be deducted for incorrect answers, it is better to guess than to omit a question.

8) Speed tests

It is often better NOT to guess on speed tests. It has been found that on timed tests people are tempted to spend the last few seconds before time is called in marking answers at random – without even reading them – in the hope of picking up a few extra points. To discourage this practice, the instructions may warn you that your score will be "corrected" for guessing. That is, a penalty will be applied. The incorrect answers will be deducted from the correct ones, or some other penalty formula will be used.

9) Review your answers

If you finish before time is called, go back to the questions you guessed or omitted to give them further thought. Review other answers if you have time.

10) Return your test materials

If you are ready to leave before others have finished or time is called, take ALL your materials to the monitor and leave quietly. Never take any test material with you. The monitor can discover whose papers are not complete, and taking a test booklet may be grounds for disqualification.

VIII. EXAMINATION TECHNIQUES

1) Read the general instructions carefully. These are usually printed on the first page of the exam booklet. As a rule, these instructions refer to the timing of the examination; the fact that you should not start work until the signal and must stop work at a signal, etc. If there are any *special* instructions, such as a choice of questions to be answered, make sure that you note this instruction carefully.

2) When you are ready to start work on the examination, that is as soon as the signal has been given, read the instructions to each question booklet, underline any key words or phrases, such as *least, best, outline, describe* and the like. In this way you will tend to answer as requested rather than discover on reviewing your paper that you *listed without describing*, that you selected the *worst* choice rather than the *best* choice, etc.

3) If the examination is of the objective or multiple-choice type – that is, each question will also give a series of possible answers: A, B, C or D, and you are called upon to select the best answer and write the letter next to that answer on your answer paper – it is advisable to start answering each question in turn. There may be anywhere from 50 to 100 such questions in the three or four hours allotted and you can see how much time would be taken if you read through all the questions before beginning to answer any. Furthermore, if you come across a question or group of questions which you know would be difficult to answer, it would undoubtedly affect your handling of all the other questions.

4) If the examination is of the essay type and contains but a few questions, it is a moot point as to whether you should read all the questions before starting to answer any one. Of course, if you are given a choice – say five out of seven and the like – then it is essential to read all the questions so you can eliminate the two that are most difficult. If, however, you are asked to answer all the questions, there may be danger in trying to answer the easiest one first because you may find that you will spend too much time on it. The best technique is to answer the first question, then proceed to the second, etc.

5) Time your answers. Before the exam begins, write down the time it started, then add the time allowed for the examination and write down the time it must be completed, then divide the time available somewhat as follows:
   - If 3-1/2 hours are allowed, that would be 210 minutes. If you have 80 objective-type questions, that would be an average of 2-1/2 minutes per question. Allow yourself no more than 2 minutes per question, or a total of 160 minutes, which will permit about 50 minutes to review.
   - If for the time allotment of 210 minutes there are 7 essay questions to answer, that would average about 30 minutes a question. Give yourself only 25 minutes per question so that you have about 35 minutes to review.

6) The most important instruction is to *read each question* and make sure you know what is wanted. The second most important instruction is to *time yourself properly* so that you answer every question. The third most important instruction is to *answer every question*. Guess if you have to but include something for each question. Remember that you will receive no credit for a blank and will probably receive some credit if you write something in answer to an essay question. If you guess a letter – say "B" for a multiple-choice question – you may have guessed right. If you leave a blank as an answer to a multiple-choice question, the examiners may respect your feelings but it will not add a point to your score. Some exams may penalize you for wrong answers, so in such cases *only*, you may not want to guess unless you have some basis for your answer.

7) Suggestions
   a. Objective-type questions
      1. Examine the question booklet for proper sequence of pages and questions
      2. Read all instructions carefully
      3. Skip any question which seems too difficult; return to it after all other questions have been answered
      4. Apportion your time properly; do not spend too much time on any single question or group of questions

5. Note and underline key words – *all, most, fewest, least, best, worst, same, opposite*, etc.
6. Pay particular attention to negatives
7. Note unusual option, e.g., unduly long, short, complex, different or similar in content to the body of the question
8. Observe the use of "hedging" words – *probably, may, most likely*, etc.
9. Make sure that your answer is put next to the same number as the question
10. Do not second-guess unless you have good reason to believe the second answer is definitely more correct
11. Cross out original answer if you decide another answer is more accurate; do not erase until you are ready to hand your paper in
12. Answer all questions; guess unless instructed otherwise
13. Leave time for review

b. Essay questions
1. Read each question carefully
2. Determine exactly what is wanted. Underline key words or phrases.
3. Decide on outline or paragraph answer
4. Include many different points and elements unless asked to develop any one or two points or elements
5. Show impartiality by giving pros and cons unless directed to select one side only
6. Make and write down any assumptions you find necessary to answer the questions
7. Watch your English, grammar, punctuation and choice of words
8. Time your answers; don't crowd material

8) Answering the essay question

Most essay questions can be answered by framing the specific response around several key words or ideas. Here are a few such key words or ideas:

M's: manpower, materials, methods, money, management
P's: purpose, program, policy, plan, procedure, practice, problems, pitfalls, personnel, public relations

a. Six basic steps in handling problems:
1. Preliminary plan and background development
2. Collect information, data and facts
3. Analyze and interpret information, data and facts
4. Analyze and develop solutions as well as make recommendations
5. Prepare report and sell recommendations
6. Install recommendations and follow up effectiveness

b. Pitfalls to avoid
1. *Taking things for granted* – A statement of the situation does not necessarily imply that each of the elements is necessarily true; for example, a complaint may be invalid and biased so that all that can be taken for granted is that a complaint has been registered

2. *Considering only one side of a situation* – Wherever possible, indicate several alternatives and then point out the reasons you selected the best one
3. *Failing to indicate follow up* – Whenever your answer indicates action on your part, make certain that you will take proper follow-up action to see how successful your recommendations, procedures or actions turn out to be
4. *Taking too long in answering any single question* – Remember to time your answers properly

IX. AFTER THE TEST

Scoring procedures differ in detail among civil service jurisdictions although the general principles are the same. Whether the papers are hand-scored or graded by machine we have described, they are nearly always graded by number. That is, the person who marks the paper knows only the number – never the name – of the applicant. Not until all the papers have been graded will they be matched with names. If other tests, such as training and experience or oral interview ratings have been given, scores will be combined. Different parts of the examination usually have different weights. For example, the written test might count 60 percent of the final grade, and a rating of training and experience 40 percent. In many jurisdictions, veterans will have a certain number of points added to their grades.

After the final grade has been determined, the names are placed in grade order and an eligible list is established. There are various methods for resolving ties between those who get the same final grade – probably the most common is to place first the name of the person whose application was received first. Job offers are made from the eligible list in the order the names appear on it. You will be notified of your grade and your rank as soon as all these computations have been made. This will be done as rapidly as possible.

People who are found to meet the requirements in the announcement are called "eligibles." Their names are put on a list of eligible candidates. An eligible's chances of getting a job depend on how high he stands on this list and how fast agencies are filling jobs from the list.

When a job is to be filled from a list of eligibles, the agency asks for the names of people on the list of eligibles for that job. When the civil service commission receives this request, it sends to the agency the names of the three people highest on this list. Or, if the job to be filled has specialized requirements, the office sends the agency the names of the top three persons who meet these requirements from the general list.

The appointing officer makes a choice from among the three people whose names were sent to him. If the selected person accepts the appointment, the names of the others are put back on the list to be considered for future openings.

That is the rule in hiring from all kinds of eligible lists, whether they are for typist, carpenter, chemist, or something else. For every vacancy, the appointing officer has his choice of any one of the top three eligibles on the list. This explains why the person whose name is on top of the list sometimes does not get an appointment when some of the persons lower on the list do. If the appointing officer chooses the second or third eligible, the No. 1 eligible does not get a job at once, but stays on the list until he is appointed or the list is terminated.

X. HOW TO PASS THE INTERVIEW TEST

The examination for which you applied requires an oral interview test. You have already taken the written test and you are now being called for the interview test – the final part of the formal examination.

You may think that it is not possible to prepare for an interview test and that there are no procedures to follow during an interview. Our purpose is to point out some things you can do in advance that will help you and some good rules to follow and pitfalls to avoid while you are being interviewed.

What is an interview supposed to test?

The written examination is designed to test the technical knowledge and competence of the candidate; the oral is designed to evaluate intangible qualities, not readily measured otherwise, and to establish a list showing the relative fitness of each candidate – as measured against his competitors – for the position sought. Scoring is not on the basis of "right" and "wrong," but on a sliding scale of values ranging from "not passable" to "outstanding." As a matter of fact, it is possible to achieve a relatively low score without a single "incorrect" answer because of evident weakness in the qualities being measured.

Occasionally, an examination may consist entirely of an oral test – either an individual or a group oral. In such cases, information is sought concerning the technical knowledges and abilities of the candidate, since there has been no written examination for this purpose. More commonly, however, an oral test is used to supplement a written examination.

Who conducts interviews?

The composition of oral boards varies among different jurisdictions. In nearly all, a representative of the personnel department serves as chairman. One of the members of the board may be a representative of the department in which the candidate would work. In some cases, "outside experts" are used, and, frequently, a businessman or some other representative of the general public is asked to serve. Labor and management or other special groups may be represented. The aim is to secure the services of experts in the appropriate field.

However the board is composed, it is a good idea (and not at all improper or unethical) to ascertain in advance of the interview who the members are and what groups they represent. When you are introduced to them, you will have some idea of their backgrounds and interests, and at least you will not stutter and stammer over their names.

What should be done before the interview?

While knowledge about the board members is useful and takes some of the surprise element out of the interview, there is other preparation which is more substantive. It *is* possible to prepare for an oral interview – in several ways:

1) Keep a copy of your application and review it carefully before the interview

This may be the only document before the oral board, and the starting point of the interview. Know what education and experience you have listed there, and the sequence and dates of all of it. Sometimes the board will ask you to review the highlights of your experience for them; you should not have to hem and haw doing it.

2) Study the class specification and the examination announcement

Usually, the oral board has one or both of these to guide them. The qualities, characteristics or knowledges required by the position sought are stated in these documents. They offer valuable clues as to the nature of the oral interview. For example, if the job involves supervisory responsibilities, the announcement will usually indicate that knowledge of modern supervisory methods and the qualifications of the candidate as a supervisor will be tested. If so, you can expect such questions, frequently in the form of a hypothetical situation which you are expected to solve. NEVER go into an oral without knowledge of the duties and responsibilities of the job you seek.

3) Think through each qualification required

Try to visualize the kind of questions you would ask if you were a board member. How well could you answer them? Try especially to appraise your own knowledge and background in each area, *measured against the job sought*, and identify any areas in which you are weak. Be critical and realistic – do not flatter yourself.

4) Do some general reading in areas in which you feel you may be weak

For example, if the job involves supervision and your past experience has NOT, some general reading in supervisory methods and practices, particularly in the field of human relations, might be useful. Do NOT study agency procedures or detailed manuals. The oral board will be testing your understanding and capacity, not your memory.

5) Get a good night's sleep and watch your general health and mental attitude

You will want a clear head at the interview. Take care of a cold or any other minor ailment, and of course, no hangovers.

What should be done on the day of the interview?

Now comes the day of the interview itself. Give yourself plenty of time to get there. Plan to arrive somewhat ahead of the scheduled time, particularly if your appointment is in the fore part of the day. If a previous candidate fails to appear, the board might be ready for you a bit early. By early afternoon an oral board is almost invariably behind schedule if there are many candidates, and you may have to wait. Take along a book or magazine to read, or your application to review, but leave any extraneous material in the waiting room when you go in for your interview. In any event, relax and compose yourself.

The matter of dress is important. The board is forming impressions about you – from your experience, your manners, your attitude, and your appearance. Give your personal appearance careful attention. Dress your best, but not your flashiest. Choose conservative, appropriate clothing, and be sure it is immaculate. This is a business interview, and your appearance should indicate that you regard it as such. Besides, being well groomed and properly dressed will help boost your confidence.

Sooner or later, someone will call your name and escort you into the interview room. *This is it.* From here on you are on your own. It is too late for any more preparation. But remember, you asked for this opportunity to prove your fitness, and you are here because your request was granted.

What happens when you go in?

The usual sequence of events will be as follows: The clerk (who is often the board stenographer) will introduce you to the chairman of the oral board, who will introduce you to the other members of the board. Acknowledge the introductions before you sit down. Do not be surprised if you find a microphone facing you or a stenotypist sitting by. Oral interviews are usually recorded in the event of an appeal or other review.

Usually the chairman of the board will open the interview by reviewing the highlights of your education and work experience from your application – primarily for the benefit of the other members of the board, as well as to get the material into the record. Do not interrupt or comment unless there is an error or significant misinterpretation; if that is the case, do not hesitate. But do not quibble about insignificant matters. Also, he will usually ask you some question about your education, experience or your present job – partly to get you to start talking and to establish the interviewing "rapport." He may start the actual questioning, or turn it over to one of the other members. Frequently, each member undertakes the questioning on a particular area, one in which he is perhaps most competent, so you can expect each member to participate in the examination. Because time is limited, you may also expect some rather abrupt switches in the direction the questioning takes, so do not be upset by it. Normally, a board member will not pursue a single line of questioning unless he discovers a particular strength or weakness.

After each member has participated, the chairman will usually ask whether any member has any further questions, then will ask you if you have anything you wish to add. Unless you are expecting this question, it may floor you. Worse, it may start you off on an extended, extemporaneous speech. The board is not usually seeking more information. The question is principally to offer you a last opportunity to present further qualifications or to indicate that you have nothing to add. So, if you feel that a significant qualification or characteristic has been overlooked, it is proper to point it out in a sentence or so. Do not compliment the board on the thoroughness of their examination – they have been sketchy, and you know it. If you wish, merely say, "No thank you, I have nothing further to add." This is a point where you can "talk yourself out" of a good impression or fail to present an important bit of information. Remember, *you close the interview yourself.*

The chairman will then say, "That is all, Mr. _____, thank you." Do not be startled; the interview is over, and quicker than you think. Thank him, gather your belongings and take your leave. Save your sigh of relief for the other side of the door.

How to put your best foot forward

Throughout this entire process, you may feel that the board individually and collectively is trying to pierce your defenses, seek out your hidden weaknesses and embarrass and confuse you. Actually, this is not true. They are obliged to make an appraisal of your qualifications for the job you are seeking, and they want to see you in your best light. Remember, they must interview all candidates and a non-cooperative candidate may become a failure in spite of their best efforts to bring out his qualifications. Here are 15 suggestions that will help you:

1) Be natural – Keep your attitude confident, not cocky

If you are not confident that you can do the job, do not expect the board to be. Do not apologize for your weaknesses, try to bring out your strong points. The board is interested in a positive, not negative, presentation. Cockiness will antagonize any board member and make him wonder if you are covering up a weakness by a false show of strength.

2) Get comfortable, but don't lounge or sprawl

Sit erectly but not stiffly. A careless posture may lead the board to conclude that you are careless in other things, or at least that you are not impressed by the importance of the occasion. Either conclusion is natural, even if incorrect. Do not fuss with your clothing, a pencil or an ashtray. Your hands may occasionally be useful to emphasize a point; do not let them become a point of distraction.

3) Do not wisecrack or make small talk

This is a serious situation, and your attitude should show that you consider it as such. Further, the time of the board is limited – they do not want to waste it, and neither should you.

4) Do not exaggerate your experience or abilities

In the first place, from information in the application or other interviews and sources, the board may know more about you than you think. Secondly, you probably will not get away with it. An experienced board is rather adept at spotting such a situation, so do not take the chance.

5) If you know a board member, do not make a point of it, yet do not hide it

Certainly you are not fooling him, and probably not the other members of the board. Do not try to take advantage of your acquaintanceship – it will probably do you little good.

6) Do not dominate the interview

Let the board do that. They will give you the clues – do not assume that you have to do all the talking. Realize that the board has a number of questions to ask you, and do not try to take up all the interview time by showing off your extensive knowledge of the answer to the first one.

7) Be attentive

You only have 20 minutes or so, and you should keep your attention at its sharpest throughout. When a member is addressing a problem or question to you, give him your undivided attention. Address your reply principally to him, but do not exclude the other board members.

8) Do not interrupt

A board member may be stating a problem for you to analyze. He will ask you a question when the time comes. Let him state the problem, and wait for the question.

9) Make sure you understand the question

Do not try to answer until you are sure what the question is. If it is not clear, restate it in your own words or ask the board member to clarify it for you. However, do not haggle about minor elements.

10) Reply promptly but not hastily

A common entry on oral board rating sheets is "candidate responded readily," or "candidate hesitated in replies." Respond as promptly and quickly as you can, but do not jump to a hasty, ill-considered answer.

11) Do not be peremptory in your answers

A brief answer is proper – but do not fire your answer back. That is a losing game from your point of view. The board member can probably ask questions much faster than you can answer them.

12) Do not try to create the answer you think the board member wants

He is interested in what kind of mind you have and how it works – not in playing games. Furthermore, he can usually spot this practice and will actually grade you down on it.

13) Do not switch sides in your reply merely to agree with a board member

Frequently, a member will take a contrary position merely to draw you out and to see if you are willing and able to defend your point of view. Do not start a debate, yet do not surrender a good position. If a position is worth taking, it is worth defending.

14) Do not be afraid to admit an error in judgment if you are shown to be wrong

The board knows that you are forced to reply without any opportunity for careful consideration. Your answer may be demonstrably wrong. If so, admit it and get on with the interview.

15) Do not dwell at length on your present job

The opening question may relate to your present assignment. Answer the question but do not go into an extended discussion. You are being examined for a *new* job, not your present one. As a matter of fact, try to phrase ALL your answers in terms of the job for which you are being examined.

Basis of Rating

Probably you will forget most of these "do's" and "don'ts" when you walk into the oral interview room. Even remembering them all will not ensure you a passing grade. Perhaps you did not have the qualifications in the first place. But remembering them will help you to put your best foot forward, without treading on the toes of the board members.

Rumor and popular opinion to the contrary notwithstanding, an oral board wants you to make the best appearance possible. They know you are under pressure – but they also want to see how you respond to it as a guide to what your reaction would be under the pressures of the job you seek. They will be influenced by the degree of poise you display, the personal traits you show and the manner in which you respond.

ABOUT THIS BOOK

This book contains tests divided into Examination Sections. Go through each test, answering every question in the margin. We have also attached a sample answer sheet at the back of the book that can be removed and used. At the end of each test look at the answer key and check your answers. On the ones you got wrong, look at the right answer choice and learn. Do not fill in the answers first. Do not memorize the questions and answers, but understand the answer and principles involved. On your test, the questions will likely be different from the samples. Questions are changed and new ones added. If you understand these past questions you should have success with any changes that arise. Tests may consist of several types of questions. We have additional books on each subject should more study be advisable or necessary for you. Finally, the more you study, the better prepared you will be. This book is intended to be the last thing you study before you walk into the examination room. Prior study of relevant texts is also recommended. NLC publishes some of these in our Fundamental Series. Knowledge and good sense are important factors in passing your exam. Good luck also helps. So now study this Passbook, absorb the material contained within and take that knowledge into the examination. Then do your best to pass that exam.

EXAMINATION SECTION

EXAMINATION SECTION
TEST 1

DIRECTIONS: Each question or incomplete statement is followed by several suggested answers or completions. Select the one that BEST answers the question or completes the statement. *PRINT THE LETTER OF THE CORRECT ANSWER IN THE SPACE AT THE RIGHT.*

1. To check for the entrance of toxic wastes into a treatment plant, each of the following may be reliably observed as indicators EXCEPT

    A. changes in color of incoming wastewater
    B. waste recording equipment
    C. odors
    D. bulking of sludge in the clarifier

    1.____

2. An increase in _____ could cause a demand for more oxygen in an aeration tank.

    A. inert or inorganic wastes
    B. pH
    C. toxic substances
    D. microorganisms

    2.____

3. Chlorine may be added for hydrogen sulfide control in the

    A. collection lines
    B. aeration tank
    C. plant effluent
    D. trickling filter

    3.____

4. The range of typical carrying capacities, in gallons per minute, of intermediate pumping stations is

    A. less than 600
    B. 200-700
    C. 100-1,600
    D. 700-10,000

    4.____

5. A low sulfanator injector vacuum reading could be caused by

    A. missing gasket
    B. high back pressure
    C. high-volume injector flow
    D. wrong orifice

    5.____

6. Before starting a rotating biological contactor process, each of the following should be checked EXCEPT

    A. lubrication
    B. biomass
    C. clearance
    D. tightness

    6.____

7. The capacity for water or wastewater to neutralize acids is expressed in terms of

    A. pH
    B. oxygen demand
    C. alkalinity
    D. acidity

    7.____

8. Which of the following is NOT one of the available methods for determining stormwater flow for the purpose of storm sewer design?

    8.____

1

A. Rainfall and runoff correlation studies
B. Inlet method
C. Hydrograph method
D. Outlet method

9. What is the term for the accumulation of residue that appears on trickling filters and must be removed periodically?

   A. Sludges   B. Slurries   C. Slugs   D. Sloughings

10. A sludge containing a high number of living organisms is referred to as

    A. raw   B. activated   C. primary   D. toxic

11. Which of the following is NOT a plant location where liquid mixing is commonly practiced?

    A. Ponds
    B. Hydraulic jumps in open channels
    C. Pipelines
    D. Venturi flumes

12. Which of the following industries releases primarily inorganic wastes in its effluent?

    A. Paper
    C. Gravel washing
    B. Petroleum
    D. Dairy

13. Which of the following collection system variables could upset a plant's activated sludge process?

    A. Discharge by industrial cleaning operations
    B. Chlorination of return sludge flows
    C. Decreases in influent flows
    D. Recycling of digester supernatant

14. The second-stage BOD is also referred to as the _____ stage.

    A. carbonaceous
    C. flocculation
    B. pretreatment
    D. nitrification

15. When organic matter decomposes to form foul-smelling products associated with the lack of free oxygen, this condition is known as

    A. shock loading
    C. sloughing
    B. septicity
    D. sidestreaming

16. Which type of bacteria has the HIGHEST optimum temperature for treatment?

    A. Mesophilic
    C. Thermophilic
    B. Cryophilic
    D. Psychrophilic

17. The COD test

    A. estimates the total oxygen consumed
    B. measures the carbon oxygen demand
    C. provides results more quickly than the BOD test
    D. measures only the nitrification oxygen demand

18. Which of the following is NOT considered a major factor that may cause variations in lab test results?

   A. The nature of the material being examined
   B. Testing equipment
   C. Sampling procedures
   D. The quantity of material being examined

19. The treatment process that MOST effectively removes suspended solids from wastewater is

   A. sedimentation
   B. flocculation
   C. skimming
   D. comminution

20. Which of the following is a thickening alternative in sludge processing?

   A. Flotation
   B. Incineration
   C. Elutriation
   D. Wet oxidation

21. The device that continuously adds the flow of wastewater into a plant is the

   A. aggregate
   B. turbidity meter
   C. titrator
   D. totalizer

22. Two types of measurement required in connection with the operation of a treatment plant are

   A. effluent and downstream
   B. temperature and dissolved oxygen
   C. in-plant and receiving water
   D. temperature and receiving water

23. You may NOT dispose of excess activated sludge waste from package plants

   A. at a nearby treatment plant
   B. by anaerobic digestion
   C. by removal by septic tank pumper
   D. by aeration in a holding tank, then deposit in a sanitary landfill

24. What is the term for the combination of activated sludge with raw wastewater in a treatment plant?

   A. Median
   B. Liquefaction
   C. Effluent
   D. Mixed liquor

25. Landfills produce poisonous _____ gas as a byproduct of decomposition.

   A. methane
   B. nitrogen
   C. chlorofluorocarbons
   D. argon

KEY (CORRECT ANSWERS)

1. B
2. D
3. A
4. D
5. B

6. B
7. C
8. D
9. D
10. B

11. A
12. C
13. A
14. D
15. B

16. C
17. C
18. D
19. B
20. A

21. D
22. C
23. B
24. D
25. A

TEST 2

DIRECTIONS: Each question or incomplete statement is followed by several suggested answers or completions. Select the one that BEST answers the question or completes the statement. *PRINT THE LETTER OF THE CORRECT ANSWER IN THE SPACE AT THE RIGHT.*

1. Which of the following types of pumps is a kinetic pump?   1.____

   A. Rotary   B. Piston plunger
   C. Hydraulic ram   D. Blow case

2. What device is used to keep floated solids out of the effluent in dissolved air flotation thickeners?   2.____

   A. Cloth screens   B. Microscreens
   C. Effluent baffles   D. Water sprays

3. The _____ is NOT one of the primary factors affecting the flow of wastewater and sewage in sewers.   3.____

   A. viscosity of the liquid
   B. cross-sectional area of the system conduit
   C. time of day
   D. pipe surface

4. What is the term for washing a digested sludge in the plant effluent?   4.____

   A. Masking   B. Elutriation
   C. Hydrolysis   D. Slaking

5. _____ is NOT an objective in periodically pumping sludge from the primary clarifier to the digester.   5.____

   A. Prevention of pump clogging
   B. Prevention of digester overload
   C. Allowance for thicker sludge pumping
   D. Maintenance of good clarifier conditions

6. The toxic chemical LEAST likely to be encountered by treatment plant operators is(are)   6.____

   A. mercury   B. acids
   C. fluorocarbons   D. bases

7. Which concentration of total dissolved solids, in milligrams per liter, would be the MINIMUM required in order to be considered *strong* in wastewater?   7.____

   A. 250   B. 500   C. 850   D. 1,200

8. What is the term for the treatment process in which a tank or reactor is filled, the water is treated, and the tank is emptied?   8.____

   A. Flocculation   B. Centration
   C. Batch process   D. Pond process

9. The mixing of a compound with water to produce a true chemical reaction is to   9.____

   A. dissolve   B. slake   C. strip   D. hydrate

10. If the difference in elevation between inflow and outflow sewers is greater than 1.5 feet, which device is needed?   10._____

    A. Side weir
    C. Baffles
    B. Drop inlet
    D. Inlet casting

11. Intermittent releases or discharges of industrial wastes are known as   11._____

    A. slurries   B. slugs   C. splashes   D. stop logs

12. Results from the settleability test of activated sludge solids may be used to   12._____

    A. calculate BOD
    B. determine probable flow rates at which sludges may clog equipment
    C. calculate sludge age
    D. determine ability of solids to separate from liquid in final clarifier

13. The device used to measure the temperature of an effluent is a   13._____

    A. thermometer
    C. thermocouple
    B. Bourdon tube
    D. pug mill

14. Which source is typically the HEAVIEST contributor of total solids in a service area's wastewater supply?   14._____

    A. Industrial wastes
    C. Storm runoff
    B. Domestic wash waters
    D. Human biological wastes

15. The term for liquid removed from a settled sludge is   15._____

    A. hydrolyte
    C. aliquot
    B. supernatant
    D. slurry

16. A unit of wastewater moving through the treatment system without dispersing or mixing with the rest of the wastewater in the system is called   16._____

    A. centration
    C. putrefaction
    B. plug flow
    D. slugging

17. What is the term for the groups or clumps of bacteria or particles that have clustered together during the treatment process?   17._____

    A. Coagulants
    C. Floes
    B. Slurries
    D. Slugs

18. The purpose of PRIMARY sedimentation is to remove   18._____

    A. settleable and floatable material
    B. roots, rags, and large debris
    C. suspended and dissolved solids
    D. sand and gravel

19. _____ would NOT cause an increase in effluent coliform levels at a treatment plant.   19._____

    A. Mixing problems
    B. An increase in effluent BOD
    C. Solids accumulation in the contact chamber
    D. High chlorine residual

20. What is the term used to describe bacteria that can live under either aerobic or anaerobic conditions?

    A. Cultured
    B. Agglomerated
    C. Filamentous
    D. Facultative

21. Which devices are NOT used during pretreatment?

    A. Racks
    B. Comminutors
    C. Screens
    D. Coagulators

22. Through which stage in an activated sludge treatment plant would wastewater pass FIRST?

    A. Grit chambers
    B. Bar racks
    C. Settling tanks
    D. Primary sedimentation

23. The inorganic gas LEAST likely to be found around a treatment plant is

    A. ammonia
    B. methane
    C. hydrogen sulfide
    D. mercaptans

24. The soils in an effluent disposal on land program may be tested using each of the following procedures EXCEPT

    A. BOD
    B. conductivity
    C. pH
    D. cation exchange capacity

25. Which of the following is a conditioning alternative in sludge processing?

    A. Centrifugation
    B. Drying
    C. Composing
    D. Elutriation

KEY (CORRECT ANSWERS)

1.	C	11.	B
2.	C	12.	D
3.	C	13.	C
4.	B	14.	A
5.	A	15.	B
6.	C	16.	B
7.	C	17.	C
8.	C	18.	A
9.	B	19.	D
10.	B	20.	D

21.	D
22.	B
23.	D
24.	A
25.	D

EXAMINATION SECTION
TEST 1

DIRECTIONS: Each question or incomplete statement is followed by several suggested answers or completions. Select the one that BEST answers the question or completes the statement. *PRINT THE LETTER OF THE CORRECT ANSWER IN THE SPACE AT THE RIGHT.*

1. To measure the diameter of a replacement pump shaft, a(n) _____ should be used. 1.____

    A. surveyor's chain
    B. micrometer
    C. metallic tape
    D. engineer's scale

2. A _____ is used to bypass storm flow in a combined-sewerage system. 2.____

    A. drop inlet
    B. side weir
    C. hydraulic jump
    D. baffle

3. The PRIMARY element in a control system is the 3.____

    A. transmitter
    B. receiver
    C. sensor
    D. controller

4. The use of water to break down complex substances into simpler ones is called 4.____

    A. dissolving
    B. hydrolysis
    C. coagulation
    D. hydrostasis

5. In its progress through a pumping station, wastewater FIRST passes through a 5.____

    A. comminutor
    B. chlorine room
    C. wet well
    D. barminutor

6. Which of the following is NOT one of the main operational factors for a barminutor? 6.____

    A. Amount of debris in wastewater
    B. Number of units in service
    C. Head loss through unit
    D. Removal of floatables

7. Which of the following precautions must be taken before attempting to repair a surface aerator? 7.____

    A. Shut down aerator
    B. Drain aeration tank
    C. Secure header assembly
    D. Test atmosphere for toxic gases

8. Which of the following source types would MOST likely influence the pH of wastewater? 8.____

    A. Industrial
    B. Commercial
    C. Agricultural
    D. Domestic

9. Each of the following items should be carefully controlled in an activated sludge plant in order to prevent sludge bulking EXCEPT 9.____

    A. filamentous growth
    B. length of aeration time
    C. return sludge rate
    D. sludge age

10. Sludge blanket depths may be measured by the use of

   A. ultrasonic transmitters and receivers
   B. pressure gages
   C. floats connected to cables
   D. bubbler tubes

11. The vertical distance from the normal water surface to the top of the confining wall of a pond or tank is called the

   A. freeboard   B. force main
   C. header   D. stop log

12. Suspended solids in the effluent from a trickling filter plant may be caused by

   A. heavy sloughing from the filters
   B. precipitation of solids in the secondary filter
   C. condensation of effluent on secondary equipment
   D. flotation of solids in the primary clarifier

13. What is MOST often produced during the decomposition of domestic wastes?

   A. Phenols   B. Oxygen
   C. Hydrogen sulfide   D. Sulfur

14. Air compressor vibration sensing devices are used to measure each of the following EXCEPT

   A. flow   B. velocity
   C. acceleration   D. displacement

15. The height or energy of liquids above a certain point is measured in terms of

   A. discharge rate   B. volume
   C. flow   D. head

16. Factors in the design of sanitary sewers include each of the following EXCEPT

   A. maximum rate for an entire service area's domestic sewage within a specified time period
   B. maximum rates from commercial and industrial areas
   C. infiltration allowance for entire service area
   D. maximum rates from domestic and industrial/commercial sources combined

17. Which of the following could prevent a pump from starting?

   A. Tripped circuit breakers
   B. Air leaks in suction line
   C. High discharge head
   D. Lack of priming

18. Through which stage would wastewater undergoing chemical-physical treatment pass FIRST?

   A. Precipitation   B. Stripping
   C. Flocculation   D. Slaking

19. Which of the following could be considered a normal operating condition for micro-screens?   19._____

    A. High flow   B. High pH level
    C. Low pH flow   D. Toxic wastes

20. The tank in which sludges are placed in order to allow decomposition is known as the   20._____

    A. emulsion   B. dessicator
    C. digester   D. percolator

21. The conversion of large solid sludge particles into fine particles that can be dissolved or suspended in water is called   21._____

    A. hydrolysis   B. liquefaction
    C. comminution   D. recirculation

22. A mixture in which two or more liquid substances are held in suspension is called a(n)   22._____

    A. solution   B. electrolyte
    C. emulsion   D. reagent

23. What is the term for a mass of sludge containing a highly concentrated population of microorganisms?   23._____

    A. Septic   B. Seed
    C. Shock load   D. Slug

24. Which of the following forms of nitrogen is LEAST important to the wastewater treatment process?   24._____

    A. Nitrate   B. Ammonia   C. Elemental   D. Organic

25. What is the term for water leaving a centrifuge after the removal of most solids?   25._____

    A. Cation exchange   B. Centration
    C. Flocculation   D. Turbidity

KEY (CORRECT ANSWERS)

1. B
2. B
3. C
4. B
5. C

6. D
7. A
8. A
9. D
10. A

11. A
12. A
13. C
14. A
15. D

16. D
17. A
18. C
19. D
20. C

21. B
22. C
23. B
24. C
25. B

TEST 2

DIRECTIONS: Each question or incomplete statement is followed by several suggested answers or completions. Select the one that BEST answers the question or completes the statement. *PRINT THE LETTER OF THE CORRECT ANSWER IN THE SPACE AT THE RIGHT.*

1. The MOST effective treatment process for destroying or removing bacteria from waste-water is through

    A. activated sludge process
    B. trickling filter
    C. chlorination
    D. sedimentation

    1.____

2. Which of the following tasks is NOT associated with the starting of a comminutor?

    A. Check positioning of inlet and outlet gases
    B. Inspect for frayed cables
    C. Adjust cutter blades
    D. Inspect for lubrication and oil leaks

    2.____

3. One of the objectives of digester mixing is

    A. the use of waste gas to run mixers
    B. adequate cooling throughout digester contents
    C. the release of hydrogen sulfide gas
    D. microorganic inoculation of raw sludge

    3.____

4. Which type of bacteria would give the STRONGEST indication of the possible presence of pathogenic bacteria in waste-water?

    A. Coliform   B. Filamentous
    C. Heterotrophic   D. Facultative

    4.____

5. Cryogenic oxygen plants should be shut down for maintenance every

    A. six months   B. year
    C. two years   D. five years

    5.____

6. At the _____ stage in the biological treatment process, aerobic bacteria uses dissolved oxygen to convert carbon compounds to carbon dioxide.

    A. clarifying   B. carbonaceous
    C. nitrification   D. coagulation

    6.____

7. _____ is NOT an influential factor in the settleability of solids in a clarifier.

    A. Detention time
    B. Flow velocity
    C. The movement of sludge scrapers
    D. Temperature

    7.____

8. Which concentration of total organic carbon, in milligrams per liter, would be considered *moderate* in wastewater?

    A. 50 B. 100 C. 200 D. 300

9. Which of the following is a volume reduction alternative in sludge processing?

    A. Centrifugation B. Chemical conditioning
    C. Flotation D. Drying

10. The hydraulic loading for a phosphate stripper depends on the

    A. dissolved oxygen of the activated sludge
    B. pH of wastewater
    C. BOD loading of the unit
    D. ability of the aerobic phosphate stripper to remain aerobic

11. The range of typical carrying capacities, in gallons per minute, of package-plant pumping stations is

    A. less than 600 B. 200-700
    C. 100-1,600 D. 700-10,000

12. When a sludge becomes too light and refuses to settle properly in a clarifier, this is known as

    A. centration B. precipitation
    C. comminution D. bulking

13. In a wet well, level control systems include each of the following EXCEPT

    A. bubblers B. hearts C. floats D. electrodes

14. Which of the following is NOT one of the primary sources of odors in a wastewater treatment plant?

    A. Unwashed grit
    B. The carbon adsorption process
    C. Sludge incinerators
    D. Waste-gas burning

15. A chemical property used in the classification of irrigation waters is

    A. pH B. total dissolved solids
    C. BOD D. aeration

16. Which of the following is NOT a potential use for the dissolved air flotation process?

    A. Solids recovery B. Coagulation
    C. Wastewater treatment D. Water recovery

17. Each of the following is a principal factor determining the use of pumping stations in sewage collection EXCEPT the

    A. elevation of the area or district to be serviced
    B. location of natural drainage areas in relation to the service area
    C. cost of a pumping station
    D. cost of trunk sewer construction

18. Through which stage would wastewater undergoing chemical-physical treatment pass LAST? 18._____

    A. Carbon adsorption
    B. Lime recovery
    C. Flocculation
    D. Slaking

19. Which of the following practices is NOT included in the maintenance of equipment in package operation plants? 19._____

    A. Changing oil in the speed reducer
    B. Adjusting aeration equipment
    C. Washing tank walls and channels
    D. Inspecting the air-lift pump

20. What chemical solution is capable of neutralizing acids or bases without greatly altering pH? 20._____
    A(n)

    A. blank   B. alkaline   C. buffer   D. digester

21. Which of the following types of pumps is a displacement pump? 21._____

    A. Centrifugal
    B. Electromagnetic
    C. Peripheral
    D. Diaphragm

22. A sludge whose solid portion can be separated from the liquid is referred to as 22._____

    A. anhydrous
    B. soluble
    C. hydrolytic
    D. dewaterable

23. Which of the following could indicate that a high organic waste load has reached the activated sludge process? 23._____
    A(n)

    A. *increase* in DO residual in the aeration tank
    B. *increase* in turbidity in the effluent from the secondary chamber
    C. *decrease* in nutrients in the effluent from the secondary chamber
    D. *decrease* in aeration

24. The term for the clogging of the filtering medium or a microscreen or a vacuum filter is 24._____

    A. corrosion
    B. head loss
    C. coagulation
    D. blinding

25. Through which stage in an activated sludge treatment plant would wastewater pass LAST? 25._____

    A. Grit chamber
    B. Chlorine contact chamber
    C. Settling tanks
    D. Trickling filters

KEY (CORRECT ANSWERS)

1. C
2. B
3. D
4. A
5. B

6. B
7. C
8. C
9. D
10. A

11. B
12. D
13. B
14. B
15. B

16. B
17. C
18. A
19. A
20. C

21. D
22. D
23. B
24. D
25. B

EXAMINATION SECTION
TEST 1

DIRECTIONS: Each question or incomplete statement is followed by several suggested answers or completions. Select the one that BEST answers the question or completes the statement. *PRINT THE LETTER OF THE CORRECT ANSWER IN THE SPACE AT THE RIGHT.*

1. The rate at which solids settle out of sewage in a sedimentation tank is dependent MAINLY on the

    A. depth of sewage in tank
    B. velocity of flow through tank
    C. water pressure
    D. amount of solids in sewage

2. Flow of sewage to the treatment plant from the intercepting sewer is controlled by a

    A. sluice gate B. flight
    C. reduction valve D. bar screen

3. The process of adding chemicals to the sewage to increase the rate of settlement of suspended solids is known as

    A. calcination B. oxydation
    C. flocculation D. chlorination

4. Large objects, such as sticks, are removed from raw sewage by a

    A. sludge pump B. settling tank
    C. bar rack D. ejector

5. Grit is MOST frequently moved from the grit chamber to the grit storage tank by

    A. gravity flow B. compressed air
    C. wheelbarrow D. conveyor belt

6. The porous plates through which air enters the aeration chamber in the activates sludge process are known as

    A. diffusers B. nozzles
    C. oxygen lances D. pressure plates

7. The *strength* of sewage is measured by determining its

    A. M.D. B. HP C. G.P.M. D. B.O.D.

8. In order to prevent digestion of sludge in sedimentation tanks, the sludge is

    A. chemically treated B. aerated
    C. continuously removed D. heated

9. One of the chemicals used to increase the rate of settling of suspended solids in sewage is

    A. bromine B. carbon C. copper D. fluorine

10. Chlorine is added to sewage to
    A. aid sludge digestion
    B. kill bacteria
    C. increase B.T.U. content of gas
    D. dewater sludge in storage tanks

11. A sewer which receives BOTH rain water and sewage from residences is known as a _____ sewer.
    A. storm   B. sanitary   C. regulated   D. combined

12. Treated sewage flowing out of the sewage treatment plant is known as the
    A. desiccant   B. decanter   C. effluent   D. waste

13. In the aerated sludge process, grease can conveniently be removed from the sewage in the
    A. wet well
    B. final sedimentation chamber
    C. grit chamber
    D. screening chamber

14. A device used to control the rate of flow of sewage is known as a
    A. weir   B. penstock   C. agitator   D. stator

15. A venturi meter is used to measure _____ of sewage.
    A. pressure
    B. temperature
    C. flow
    D. depth

16. Sludge gas is composed MAINLY of
    A. methane
    B. carbon monoxide
    C. hydrogen sulfide
    D. ammonia

17. Overloads on reciprocating pumps can be prevented by _____ valves.
    A. check   B. relief   C. gate   D. globe

18. A valve that permits flow in only one direction is a _____ valve.
    A. check   B. plug   C. gate   D. globe

19. Where a quick closing action is desired, the type of valve that should be used is a(n)
    A. globe   B. needle   C. gate   D. angle

20. The one of the following types of valves that causes the LEAST resistance to the flow of sewage is a(n)
    A. globe   B. angle   C. gate   D. key

21. Cavitation (pitting) in centrifugal pumps would MOST probably occur in the
    A. packing glands
    B. roller bearings
    C. pump impellers
    D. shaft

22. The type of pump MOST commonly used to pump sludge is the   22._____

    A. turbine
    B. centrifugal
    C. volute
    D. reciprocating

23. If the bearings on a large pump become excessively hot, the BEST thing to do is to   23._____

    A. pour cold water on the bearings to cool them
    B. fill the oil cup and slow the pump till the bearings cool
    C. stop the motor and check the condition of the bearings and oil or grease
    D. shunt the suction and discharge valves till the pump cools, then reopen valves slowly

24. Priming is MOST frequently required in a _____ pump.   24._____

    A. centrifugal
    B. reciprocating
    C. rotary
    D. gear

25. When gland nuts on a sewage pump are properly tightened,   25._____

    A. there will be slight leakage through the packing
    B. the packing is not compressed
    C. the lantern will rotate
    D. the stuffing box cannot overheat

KEY (CORRECT ANSWERS)

1.	B	11.	D
2.	A	12.	C
3.	C	13.	B
4.	C	14.	A
5.	B	15.	C
6.	A	16.	A
7.	D	17.	B
8.	C	18.	A
9.	C	19.	C
10.	B	20.	C

21. C
22. D
23. C
24. A
25. A

TEST 2

DIRECTIONS: Each question or incomplete statement is followed by several suggested answers or completions. Select the one that BEST answers the question or completes the statement. *PRINT THE LETTER OF THE CORRECT ANSWER IN THE SPACE AT THE RIGHT.*

1. The rated capacity of a pump is usually given in terms of

    A. horsepower and velocity of flow
    B. gallons per minute pumped and pressure head
    C. electrical consumption and velocity of flow
    D. electrical consumption and gallons per minute pumped

    1.____

2. Sudden shutting of the discharge valve of a centrifugal pump may damage a piping system because

    A. the impellers will turn for a short period without lubrication
    B. there will be leakage past the packing
    C. pump bearings will be scored
    D. water hammer will occur

    2.____

3. The one of the following that is used on a piece of mechanical equipment to prevent overloading is a

    A. bushing   B. shear pin
    C. split ring   D. yoke

    3.____

4. Sewage has suddenly stopped flowing from a centrifugal pump which has been working well.
The MOST probable cause for this is that

    A. air is leaking into suction line
    B. the bearings are worn
    C. the speed of pump is excessive
    D. the oil level is inadequate

    4.____

5. The MOST viscous of the following lubricants is

    A. diesel oil   B. cup grease
    C. S.A.E. 40 oil   D. kerosene

    5.____

6. The BEST method of lubricating roller bearings if by means of

    A. light machine oil   B. instrument oil
    C. diesel oil   D. grease

    6.____

7. A pipe reducer would be used to

    A. permit drawing of low pressure gas from high pressure pipes
    B. connect two lines of different sizes
    C. compress packing in a line expansion joint
    D. remove excess water from sludge lines

    7.____

8. The one of the following that is NOT a standard pipe fitting is a 8.____

   A. union B. tap C. tee D. cross

9. Water hammer can be reduced by using a(n) 9.____

   A. quick closing valve B. air chamber
   C. flanged connection D. automatic primer

10. To be watertight, the faces of a flanged connection should be 10.____

    A. machined
    B. packed with waste
    C. coated with rubber cement
    D. etched

11. When tightening bolts on a flanged connection, the PROPER procedure is to 11.____

    A. take up each bolt wrench hard before beginning to tighten next adjacent bolt
    B. first take up one bolt wrench hard, then tighten diagonally opposite bolt wrench hard
    C. take up each bolt gradually, tightening adjacent bolts in order
    D. take up each bolt gradually, first tightening one bolt slightly, then the diagonally opposite bolt in a like manner

12. The kind of wrench used to tighten pipe would be a(n) 12.____

    A. crescent B. open end C. monkey D. Stillson

13. The one of the following fire extinguisher types that should be used on a fire in an electric motor is 13.____

    A. carbon dioxide B. soda acid
    C. water fog D. foam

14. A safety device used to protect electrical circuits from overloads is a(n) 14.____

    A. solenoid B. powerstat
    C. circuit breaker D. transformer

15. The one of the following that is the MOST common reason for noisy operation of electric motors is 15.____

    A. shorted windings B. worn brushes
    C. worn bearings D. overloading

16. The unit of measurement used for determining the amount of energy consumed in running a motor is 16.____

    A. volt-amperes B. kilowatt hours
    C. horsepower D. frequency-cycle

17. The one of the following parts of an electric motor that will wear out MOST frequently is(are) the 17.____

    A. armature B. field pieces
    C. shaft D. brushes

18. The MOST important reason for using a fuse in an electrical circuit is to prevent excessive 18._____

    A. voltage B. current
    C. frequency D. resistance

19. An electrical device used to increase line voltage is a(n) 19._____

    A. alternator B. magneto
    C. transformer D. choke

20. The minimum size wire that should be used to supply power to a 1 H.P. motor is 20._____

    A. #14 B. #16 C. #18 D. #20

21. The one of the following that should be used to clean a commit at or is 21._____

    A. sandpaper B. emery paper
    C. pumice D. emery cloth

22. To clean armature windings on a motor, one should use 22._____

    A. calcium chloride B. sodium chloride
    C. carbon tetrachloride D. sodium hypochlorite

23. When starting an electrically driven centrifugal pump, the starting load can be reduced by 23._____

    A. opening the suction and discharge valves
    B. opening the suction valve and closing the discharge valves
    C. closing the suction and discharge valves
    D. closing the suction valve and opening the discharge valves

24. For increased safety, the frame of an electric motor should be 24._____

    A. grounded B. shorted C. shunted D. painted

25. The one of the following materials that is MOST suitable for piping corrosive sludge gas is 25._____

    A. copper B. steel C. aluminum D. transite

KEY (CORRECT ANSWERS)

1. B
2. D
3. B
4. A
5. B

6. D
7. B
8. B
9. B
10. A

11. D
12. D
13. A
14. C
15. C

16. B
17. D
18. B
19. C
20. A

21. A
22. C
23. B
24. A
25. D

EXAMINATION SECTION
TEST 1

DIRECTIONS: Answer the following questions directly, briefly, and succinctly.

Questions 1-10.

DIRECTIONS: What is the purpose of each of the following pieces of equipment in sewage treatment?

1. Coarse racks
2. Fine bar screens
3. Fine screens
4. Screening grinders
5. Grit chambers
6. Grit washers
7. Settling tanks
8. Aeration tanks
9. Sludge digesters
10. Sluice gates or weirs

Questions 11-20.

DIRECTIONS: What are the chief causes for each of the following pieces of equipment becoming defective? For each cause, indicate how you would repair the defect.

11. Mechanical screens
12. Screening grinders
13. Grit collectors
14. Grit washers
15. Main sewage and circulating pumps
16. Sludge pumps
17. Settling tanks
18. Aeration tanks
19. Sluice gates
20. Storage tanks

25

Questions 21-25.

21. What safety precaution should you take when making repairs on electric equipment?
22. What safety precaution should you take when making repairs on a mechanical rack?
23. What safety precaution should you take when grinding tools?
24. What safety precaution should you take when working with digester gas?
25. What safety precaution should you take when handling a leaking chlorine cylinder?

Questions 26-30.

26. How is grit removed from grit channels?
27. What should be done to protect flocculator mechanism in case of accumulation of grit and sand in the flocculators?
28. What is the usual period of detention in settling tanks?
29. Indicate, on a simple sketch, the direction of flow in settling tanks in use in the city.
30. What must be done in order to prevent digestion of sludge in settling tanks?

Questions 31-35.

31. In chemical precipitation, in what form are chemicals received for mixing with the sewage to increase settling?
32. In the activated sludge process, what is mixed with the raw or clarified sewage?
33. Where, in the activated sludge process, are diffuser blocks used?
34. Why is chlorine added to effluent discharging from some sewage treatment plants into bodies of water?
35. How are sludge digestion tanks heated?

Questions 36-40.

36. What is the average period of sludge detention in primary tanks?
37. What happens to sludge volume in secondary tanks?
38. What is usually done with the digested sludge resulting from plant operation?
39. What use is made of skimmings from settling tanks?
40. At what point in the activated sludge process is the sample for checking residual oxygen taken?

Questions 41-45.

41. For what is a venturi motor used?
42. What type of pump is generally used for pumping raw sewage?

43. What type of pump is generally used for pumping sludge?

44. How should electric motors be cleaned?

45. What type of fire extinguisher should be used for fires on electrical equipment?

Questions 46-50.

46. Assume that you are pumping water into a tank at the rate of 200 gallons per minute and that you are withdrawing water at the rate of 75 gallons per minute. How long will it take to add 60,000 gallons of water to the tank?

47.

The figures above show two readings of a watt-hour meter taken twenty-four hours apart. How many k.w. hours were used in that period?

4 (#1)

KEY (CORRECT ANSWERS)

1. Remove coarse materials – cans, ashes, rags, timber, etc.

2. Remove smaller materials that go through coarse racks

3. Remove particles of sewage and fine floating material (screens also protect equipment of plant through which sewage must pass)

4. Reduce size of removed particles

5. Catch sand, gravel, ashes, and other gritty material

6. Remove odor-producing materials from the grit

7. Settle out materials in sewage (sludge)

8. Treat sewage by application of air

9. Digest sludge and produce gas

10. Control and measure flow of sewage

11. Overloading causes breakage of cables, chains, shear pins. Repair by removing cause of overload and replacing broken part.

12. Overloading through delivery of too much material or dulling of knives. Repair by opening grinder, removing obstructing material, and replacing or reversing knives.

13. Moving parts – chains, shoes, pins, sprockets, flights – becoming worn. Repair by replacing worn parts.

14. Clogging of slide valves. Repair by cleaning and replacing pipe fittings. Clean, repair, and adjust such parts as chains and diaphragms.

15. Motor failure. Report to plant engineer. Loss of prime and leakage. Adjust or replace packing, adjust water seal, and reprime.

16. Obstruction under valves, over-load, slogging or leaks. Repair by replacing faulty gaskets and worn packing for air leaks, to remove obstructions, take off valve covers, and clean.

17. Same as 13

18. Plates or valves becoming clogged or broken. Service valves, clean and replace clogged or broken plates.

19. Gate skewed or jammed, spindle bent, gears jammed or broken. Re-adjust or replace.

20. Same as 14.

21. Make sure power is off and equipment grounded

22. Make sure equipment cannot be set in motion

23. Wear goggles

24. Use proper mask, keep flame away

25. Wear special gas mask and rubber gloves

26. Longitudinal or revolving scrapers

27. Periodic flushing

28. One to two hours

29.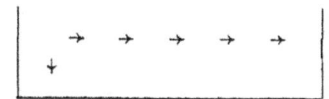

30. Continuous removal of settled sludge

31. Powder, dry with chlorine

32. Biologically active sludge, air (1/2)

33. Base of aeration tanks

34. Reduces harmful bacteria, minimizes disagreeable odors

35. Heat provided by circulating warm water through coils in the tanks

36. 20 days approximately for primary digestion tanks or 2 hours for primary settling tanks

37. Compacted to about 50% of original volume

38. Dumped at sea or used as landfill

39. Sold as fat

40. Between aeration tank and secondary settlement tank or at outlet of secondary settling tank

41. Measure flow of water

42. Centrifugal pump

43. Piston or reciprocating pump

44. Carbon tetrachloride, compressed air, rags (not waste)

45. CO_2, fire foam, carbon tetrachloride

46. 8 hours

47. 6583 or 6583
     4128   4129
     2455 or 2454

EXAMINATION SECTION
TEST 1

DIRECTIONS: Each question or incomplete statement is followed by several suggested answers or completions. Select the one that *BEST* answers the question or completes the statement. *PRINT THE LETTER OF THE CORRECT ANSWER IN THE SPACE AT THE RIGHT.*

1. In a modification of the conventional activated sludge process known as Modified Aeration, the percentage of returned sludge to the aeration tank is, MOST nearly, 1.____

    A. 10 B. 20 C. 30 D. 40

2. The amount of chlorine, in pounds per million gallons, to produce 0.5 ppm residual in most primary effluents will, *most nearly,* be between 2.____

    A. 10 to 40 B. 50 to 70 C. 100 to 200 D. 300 to 500

3. In a conventional activated sludge treatment plant, air is applied at a rate of, most *nearly,* 3.____

    A. 1 to 1 1/2 cubic feet per gallon of sewage
    B. 3 to 3 1/2 cubic feet per gallon of sewage
    C. 4 to 5 1/2 cubic feet per gallon of sewage
    D. 7 to 7 1/2 cubic feet per gallon of sewage

4. Of the following temperature ranges, the *one* which is the *MOST* efficient for sludge digester operation is 4.____

    A. 45° F and 50° F B. 55° F and 65° F
    C. 70° F and 75° F D. 85° F and 95° F

5. The sewage detention time in an aeration tank using modified aeration is, *most nearly,* 5.____

    A. 2 hours B. 4 hours C. 6 hours D. 8 hours

6. The BTU per cubic foot value of sludge gas from a well established and properly operated digestion tank is, most *nearly,* 6.____

    A. 150 B. 350 C. 450 D. 650

7. BOD is an abbreviation for 7.____

    A. Bacteria Operating Demand
    B. Biosorption Operating Demand
    C. Biochemical Oxygen Demand
    D. Biofilter Oxygen Demand

8. The one of the following that is normally used to control the flow of sewage to the treatment plant from the intercepting sewer is the 8.____

    A. float valve B. sluice gate
    C. gate valve D. regulator gate

2 (#1)

9. A sludge gas encountered at sewage treatment plants that is corrosive and damaging to metals is

   A. carbon dioxide
   B. ethane
   C. nitrogen
   D. hydrogen sulphide

10. When sludge is withdrawn from a sludge gas collector tank with a fixed color, a compensating volume of fresh sludge or water or gas must be put into the tank to prevent the development of

    A. leakage
    B. positive pressures
    C. negative pressures
    D. condensation

11. Devices in sewage treatment plants whose function is to break or cut up solids found in sewage are known as

    A. barmimutors
    B. diffusers
    C. tricklers
    D. grinders

12. The sludge treatment process whereby the volume of sludge going to the digester is reduced is known as

    A. thickening
    B. elutriation
    C. chemical conditioning
    D. wet oxidation

13. *Most* of the suspended solids are separated or removed from the sewage by

    A. aeration   B. washing   C. elutriation   D. sedimentation

14. The *one* of the following that is usually operated by compressed air is a

    A. reducer
    B. baffle
    C. sump pump
    D. sewage ejector

15. The PRIMARY function of a grit chamber in a sewage treatment plant is to remove

    A. paper   B. worms   C. gravel   D. algae

16. A deep two-storied storage sewage tank with an upper sedimentaton chamber and a lower chamber is known as a _____ tank.

    A. detritus   B. imhoff   C. septic   D. elocculating

17. The *one* of the following which BEST characterizes activated sludge is that it is

    A. black in color and has small particles
    B. blue in color and has large particles
    C. brown in color and has some dissolved oxygen
    D. beige in color and has a great amount of dissolved oxygen

18. The *optimum* PH value of the sludge in a digester should be

    A. 10   B. 7   C. 3   D. 2

19. In the Activated Sludge Process, the *one* of the following steps that may be taken to prevent or control sludge bulkings is to

    A. decrease aeration in time and rate
    B. chlorinate returned activated sludge

C. increase the solids content carried in aeration tanks
D. raise the pH value to 7.8

20. In starting a digester unit, the QUICKEST results can be obtained by

    A. seeding   B. shredding   C. dosing   D. chlorinating

21. Sludge digestion carried out in the absence of free oxygen is known as

    A. wet oxidation
    B. heat drying
    C. anaerobic decomposition
    D. aerobic decomposition

22. "Frothing" is MOST frequently attributable to

    A. short circuiting of aeration tanks
    B. septic sewage in primary tank
    C. high concentration of fungus
    D. detergent compounds in the sewage

23. The process of removing floating grease or scum from the surface of sewage in a tank is called

    A. squeegeeing
    B. siphoning
    C. skimming
    D. sloughing

24. Of the following, the one which BEST represents a primary treatment device for sewage is the

    A. stabilization pond
    B. intermittent sand filter
    C. septic tank
    D. aeration tank

25. Freshly poured concrete surfaces normally exposed to air should be cured for a minimum period of

    A. 4 days   B. 5 days   C. 6 days   D. 7 days

26. One of your men on the job is injured at a work site and is unconscious. The BEST course of action for you to follow is to

    A. give him liquids to drink
    B. have him remain in a lying position until medical help arrives
    C. immediately move him to the first-aid station
    D. attempt to arouse him to consciousness by shaking him

27. The type of portable fire extinguisher that is MOST effective in controlling a fire around live electrical equipment is the

    A. foam type
    B. soda-acid type
    C. carbon-dioxide type
    D. water type

28. The hazards of electric shock resulting from operation of a portable electric tool in a damp location can be reduced by

    A. grounding the tool
    B. holding the tool with one hand
    C. running the tool at low speed
    D. using a baffle

29. The *one* of the following that is the *proper* first aid to administer to a conscious person suffering from chlorine inhalation is 29.___

    A. an alocholic drink
    B. black coffee
    C. a pulmotor
    D. a cold shower

30. Of the following actions, the *best one* to take *FIRST* after smoke is seen coming from an electric control device is to 30.___

    A. shut off the power to it
    B. call the main office for advice
    C. look for a wiring diagram
    D. throw water on it

KEY (CORRECT ANSWERS)

1.	A	16.	B
2.	C	17.	C
3.	A	18.	B
4.	D	19.	B
5.	A	20.	A
6.	D	21.	C
7.	C	22.	D
8.	B	23.	C
9.	D	24.	C
10.	C	25.	D
11.	A	26.	B
12.	A	27.	C
13.	D	28.	A
14.	D	29.	B
15.	C	30.	A

TEST 2

DIRECTIONS: Each question or incomplete statement is followed by several suggested answers or completions. Select the one that *BEST* answers the question or completes the statement. *PRINT THE LETTER OF THE CORRECT ANSWER IN THE SPACE AT THE RIGHT.*

1. Of the following, the *BEST* fastener to use when attaching a pipe support bracket to a concrete wall is a(n) 1.____
   - A. toggle bolt
   - B. expansion bolt
   - C. carriage bolt
   - D. lag bolt

2. The *MAIN* reason for mixing a "thinner" into paint is to 2.____
   - A. *clear up* air bubbles
   - B. *stop* the paint from bleeding
   - C. *spread* the paint easily
   - D. *make* the paint color lighter

3. Schedule 40 pipe is a designation for 3.____
   - A. asbestos cement pipe
   - B. steel pipe
   - C. transite pipe
   - D. clay pipe

4. The function of a check valve in a pipeline is to 4.____
   - A. relieve excessive pressure
   - B. remove air
   - C. meter the flow
   - D. prevent reverse flow

5. The device on an electric motor which will prevent overheating is called a 5.____
   - A. rheostat
   - B. bus bar
   - C. solenoid
   - D. thermal relay

6. The oil recommended for the gear box of a 20-ton sewage plant crane is, *most nearly*, 6.____
   - A. SAE 80
   - B. SAE 120
   - C. SAE 160
   - D. SAE 200

7. Where pump ball bearings may be subjected to water washing, the lubricating grease should have a 7.____
   - A. white lead base
   - B. red lead base
   - C. sodium soap base
   - D. lithum soap base

8. A chlorine leak can normally be detected by 8.____
   - A. a lighted candle
   - B. its smell
   - C. a dry rag
   - D. an oil-soaked rag

9. The moving wooden planks in a tank used to scrape sludge from the bottom of a tank are known as 9.____
   - A. cleats
   - B. flights
   - C. rails
   - D. levers

10. A device with an edge or notch used for measuring liquid flow is known as a 10.____
    - A. Parshall Flume
    - B. Plainer Bowlus
    - C. Venturi
    - D. Weir

11. The *one* of the following types of pumps that is WIDELY used for pumping sewage is

    A. reciprocating B. rotary C. simplex D. centrifugal

12. Prior to starting a newly installed pump, you should

    A. open the motor disconnect switch
    B. expose the pump to outside weather conditions
    C. turn the shaft by hand to see that it rotates freely
    D. disconnect the vent and drain the plugs

13. A maintenance program for a new piece of operating equipment should BEST be set up in accordance with the

    A. location of the unit
    B. location of personnel
    C. manufacturer's recommendations
    D. monthly plant capacity

14. The *one* of the following fasteners that has threads at *both* ends is called a

    A. screw B. stud C. blivet D. drift bolt

15. The *one* of the following that is installed between two pipe flanges to seal the connection is called a

    A. sheave B. gasket C. boss D. fillet

16. A wet undigested sludge containing a large amount of grease will MOST probably

    A. clog the opening of the filter
    B. have no effect on the efficiency of the filters
    C. cause rapid deterioration of the filter
    D. cause the filter to shrink and snap

17. The floating cover for a sludge gas storage tank is kept under a gauge pressure of, *most nearly*,

    A. 0 to 2 ounces
    B. 3 to 5 ounces
    C. 6 to 9 ounces
    D. 10 to 12 ounces

18. The tool that is used to remove the burrs from the end of 1/2" diameter steel pipe after cutting it with a pipe cutter is known as a

    A. bit B. reamer C. tap D. caliper

19. Of the following common obstructions found in sewer lines, the *one* that occurs MOST frequently is

    A. roots B. debris C. grease D. grit

20. The *one* of the following that is the MAIN reason for putting orders in writing is to

    A. protect the person who receives it
    B. protect the person who prepared the order
    C. make it easier to check mistakes
    D. protect the agency should something unforeseen occur

21. For records to provide an essential basis for future changes or expansions of the sewage treatment plant, the records must be

   A. accurate
   B. lengthy
   C. detailed in ink
   D. hand-written in pencil

21.____

22. The volume, in cubic feet, of a slab of concrete that is 5'-0" wide, 6'-0" long, and 0'-6" in depth is, *most nearly,*

   A. 15.0   B. 13.5   C. 12.0   D. 10.5

22.____

23. The sum of the following pipe lengths, 22 1/8", 7 3/4", 19 7/16", and 4 3 5/8", is:

   A. 91 7/8"   B. 92 1/16"   C. 92 1/4"   D. 92 15/16"

23.____

24. The area in square feet of a plant floor that is 42 feet wide and 75 feet long is

   A. 3150   B. 3100   C. 3075   D. 2760

24.____

25. Of the following types of gauges, the *one* that indicates pressure above and below atmospheric pressures is known as a

   A. pressure   B. vacuum   C. Bourdan   D. compound

25.____

26. A U-tube manometer is used to measure

   A. deflection   B. height   C. radiation   D. pressure

26.____

27. If an air-conditioning unit shorted out and caught fire, the BEST fire extinguisher to use would be a _____ extinguisher.

   A. water
   B. foam
   C. carbon dioxide
   D. soda acid

27.____

28. Of the following, the *best* action to take to help someone whose eyes have been splashed with lye is to FIRST

   A. wash out the eyes with clean water
   B. wash out the eyes with a salt water solution
   C. apply a sterile dressing over the eyes
   D. do nothing to the eyes, but telephone for medical help

28.____

Questions 29-30.

DIRECTIONS: Questions numbered 29 and 30 are to be answered in accordance with the information given in the following paragraph:

A sludge lagoon is an excavated area in which digested sludge is desired. Lagoon depths vary from six to eight feet. There are no established criteria for the required capacity of a lagoon. The sludge moisture content is reduced by evaporation and drainage. Volume reduction is slow, especially in cold and rainy weather. Weather and soil conditions affect concentration. The drying period ranges from a period of several months to several years. After the sludge drying period has ended, a bulldozer or tractor can be used to remove the sludge. The dried sludge can be used for fill of low ground. A filled dried lagoon can be developed into a lawn. Lagoons can be used for emergency storage when the sludge beds are full. Lagoons are popular because they are inexpensive to build and operate. They have a disadvantage of being unsightly. A hazard to lagoon operation is the possibility of draining partly digested sludge to the lagoon that creates a fly and odor nuisance.

29. In accordance with the given paragraph, sludge lagoons have the *disadvantage* of being 29._____

    A. unsightly   B. too deep
    C. concentrated   D. wet

30. In accordance with the given paragraph, moisture content is *reduced* by 30._____

    A. digestion   B. evaporation
    C. oxidation   D. removal

KEY (CORRECT ANSWERS)

1.	B	16.	A
2.	C	17.	B
3.	B	18.	B
4.	D	19.	A
5.	D	20.	B
6.	B	21.	A
7.	D	22.	A
8.	B	23.	D
9.	B	24.	A
10.	D	25.	D
11.	D	26.	D
12.	C	27.	C
13.	C	28.	A
14.	B	29.	A
15.	A	30.	B

EXAMINATION SECTION
TEST 1

DIRECTIONS: Each question or incomplete statement is followed by several suggested answers or completions. Select the one that *BEST* answers the question or completes the statement. *PRINT THE LETTER OF THE CORRECT ANSWER IN THE SPACE AT THE RIGHT.*

1. When 60,987 is added to 27,835, the result is   1.____
   A. 80,712   B. 80,822   C. 87,712   D. 88,822

2. The sum of 693 + 787 + 946 + 355 + 731 is   2.____
   A. 3,512   B. 3,502   C. 3,412   D. 3,402

3. When 2,586 is subtracted from 3,003, the result is   3.____
   A. 417   B. 527   C. 1,417   D. 1,527

4. When 1.32 is subtracted from 52.6, the result is   4.____
   A. 3.94   B. 5.128   C. 39.4   D. 51.28

5. When 56 is multiplied by 438, the result is   5.____
   A. 840   B. 4,818   C. 24,528   D. 48,180

6. When 8.7 is multiplied by .34, the result is, most nearly,   6.____
   A. 2.9   B. 3.0   C. 29.5   D. 29.6

7. When 1/2 is divided by 2/3, the result is   7.____
   A. 1/3   B. 3/4   C. 1 1/3   D. 3

8. When 8,340 is divided by 38, the result is, most nearly   8.____
   A. 210   B. 218   C. 219   D. 220

Questions 9-11.

DIRECTIONS: Questions 9 to 11 inclusive are to be answered *SOLELY* on the basis of the information given below.

Assume that a certain water treatment plant has consumed quantities of chemicals E and F over a five-week period, as indicated in the following table:

Time Period	Number of 100-pound sacks consumed	
	Chemical E	Chemical F
Week 1	5	4
Week 2	7	5
Week 3	6	5
Week 4	8	6
Week 5	6	4

9. The *total* number of pounds of chemical E consumed at the end of the first three weeks is   9._____

    A. 180   B. 320   C. 1,400   D. 1,800

10. According to the table, the week in which the *most* chemicals were consumed was   10._____

    A. week 2   B. week 3   C. week 4   D. week 5

11. According to the table, the *average* number of sacks of chemical F consumed over the first four weeks was   11._____

    A. 4   B. 5   C. 6   D. 7

12. Of the following actions, the *best* one to take *FIRST* after smoke is seen coming from an electric control device is to   12._____

    A. shut off the power to it
    B. call the main office for advice
    C. look for a wiring diagram
    D. throw water on it

13. Of the following items, the one which would *LEAST* likely be included on a memorandum is the   13._____

    A. home address of the writer of the memorandum
    B. name of the writer of the memorandum
    C. subject of the memorandum
    D. names or titles of the person who will receive the memorandum

14. When testing joints for leaks in pipe lines containing natural gas, it is *BEST* to use   14._____

    A. water in the lines under pressure
    B. a lighted candle
    C. an aquastat
    D. soapy water

Questions 15-17.

DIRECTIONS: Questions 15 to 17 inclusive are to be answered *SOLELY* on the basis of the information given below.

Assume that at various hours of a typical day the amounts of chlorine residual in parts per million (ppm) at a certain water treatment plant are as shown in the following graph:

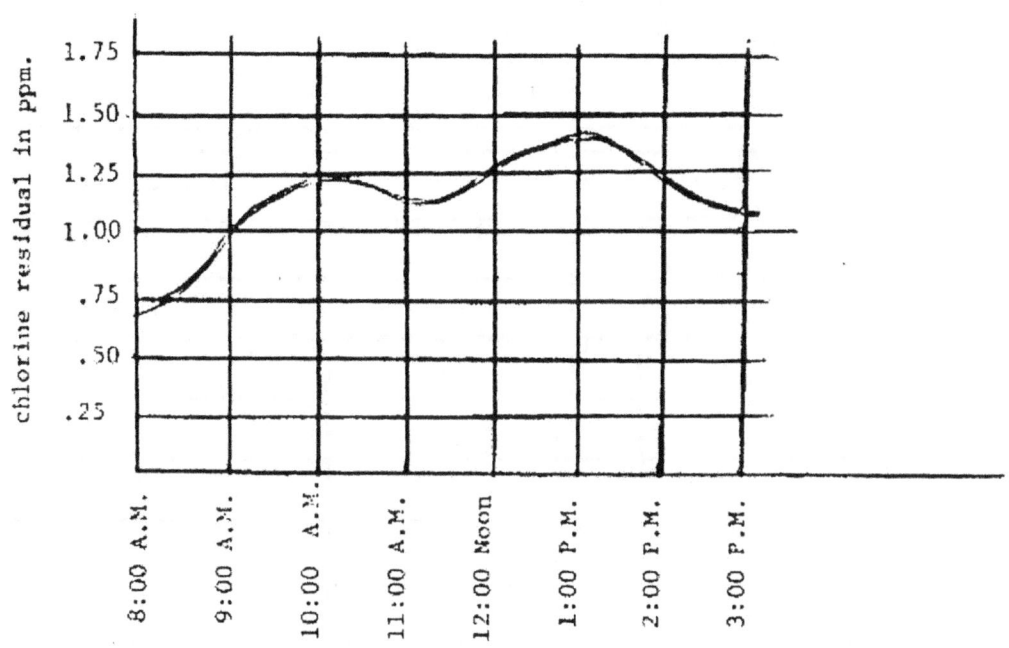

15. According to the graph, the chlorine residual measured in ppm at 9:00 A.M. was, most nearly, 15.____

    A. .70 B. .75 C. 1.00 D. 1.25

16. The maximum chlorine residual between 8:00 A.M. and 3:00 P.M. was, most nearly, 16.____

    A. .68 ppm B. 1.10 ppm C. 1.25 ppm D. 1.37 ppm

17. According to the graph, between the hour of 12:00 Noon and 1:00 P.M., the chlorine residual was 17.____

    A. always increasing
    B. always decreasing
    C. increasing, then decreasing
    D. decreasing, then increasing

18. Of the following statements concerning the use and care of wooden ladders, the *one* which is *TRUE* is that 18.____

    A. a light oil should be applied to the rungs to preserve the wood
    B. each rung should be sharply struck with a metal hammer to test its soundness before using it
    C. ladders should be stored in a warm damp area to prevent the wood from getting brittle
    D. tops of ordinary stepladders should not be used as steps

19. It is *poor* practice to use gasoline to clean metal parts that are coated with grease *PRIMARILY* because gasoline 19.____

    A. contains lead which is harmful to the user
    B. is a poor solvent for grease
    C. corrodes metal
    D. vapors ignite easily

Questions 20-21.

DIRECTIONS   Questions 20 and 21 are to be answered *SOLELY* on the basis of the information given in the tables below.

Inventory of 100 pound bags on hand as of 1-1	
Chemical X	16 1/2
Chemical Y	12

Date	Chemical	Number of 100 pound bags used	Number of 100 pound bags received
1-5	X	8 1/2	
1-9	X	3 1/2	
1-9	Y	5	
1-16	X		8
1-18	Y	2 1/2	
1-23	X	3	
1-27	Y	4 1/2	
1-30	X		2
1-31	X	1	

Inventory of 100 pound bags on hand as of 1-31	
Chemical X	
Chemical Y	

J. Doe   2-2
Operator

20. According to the information given in the table, the number of 100-pound bags of chemical Y *on hand* as of 1-31 is   20.____

    A. 0   B. 1/2   C. 1   D. 1 1/2

21. According to the information in the table, the *total* number of pounds of chemical X consumed in the month was, most nearly,   21.____

    A. 500   B. 1,600   C. 1,800   D. 2,800

Questions 22-27.

DIRECTIONS: Questions 22 to 27 inclusive are to be answered SOLELY on the basis of the paragraph below.

FIRST AID INSTRUCTIONS

The main purpose of first aid is to put the injured person in the best possible position until medical help arrives. This includes the performance of emergency treatment for the purpose of saving a life if a doctor is not present. When a person is hurt, a crowd usually gathers around the victim. If nobody uses his head, the injured person fails to get the care he needs. You must stay calm and, most important, it is your duty to take charge at an accident. The first thing for you to do is to see, as best you can, what is wrong with the injured person. Leave the victim where he is until the nature and extent of his injury are determined. If he is unconscious he should not be moved except to lay him flat on his back if he is in some other position. Loosen the clothing of any seriously hurt person and make him as comfortable as possible. Medical help should be called as soon as possible. You should remain with the injured person and send someone else to call the doctor. You should try to make sure that the one who calls for a doctor is able to give correct information as to the location of the injured person. In order to help the physician to know what equipment may be needed in each particular case, the person making the call should give the doctor as much information about the injury as possible.

22. If nobody uses his head at the scene of an accident, there is danger that

   A. no one will get the names of all the witnesses
   B. a large crowd will gather
   C. the victim will not get the care he needs
   D. the victim will blame the City for negligence

23. When an accident occurs, the FIRST thing you should do is

   A. call a doctor
   B. loosen the clothing of the injured person
   C. notify the victim's family
   D. try to find out what is wrong with the injured person

24. If you do NOT know the extent and nature of the victim's injuries, you should

   A. let the injured person lie where he is
   B. immediately take the victim to a hospital yourself
   C. help the injured person to his feet to see if he can walk
   D. have the injured person sit up on the ground while you examine him

25. If the injured person is breathing and unconscious, you should

   A. get some hot liquid such as coffee or tea in to him
   B. give him artificial respiration
   C. lift up his head to try to stimulate blood circulation
   D. see that he lies flat on his back

26. If it is necessary to call a doctor, you should 26.____

    A. go and make the call yourself since you have all the information
    B. find out who the victim's family doctor is before making the call
    C. have someone else make the call who knows the location of the victim
    D. find out which doctor the victim can afford

27. It is important for the caller to give the doctor as much information as is available regarding the injury so that the doctor 27.____

    A. can bring the necessary equipment
    B. can make out an accident report
    C. will be responsible for any malpractice resulting from the first aid treatment
    D. can inform his nurse on how long he will be in the field

Questions 28-29.

DIRECTIONS: Questions 28 and 29 are to be answered *SOLELY* on the basis of the paragraph below.

When a written report must be submitted by an operator to his supervisor, the best rule is "the briefer the better." Obviously, this can be carried to extremes, since all necessary information must be included. However, the ability to write a satisfactory one-page report is an important communication skill. There are several different kinds of reports in common use. One is the form report, which is printed and merely requires the operator to fill in blanks. The greatest problems faced in completion of this report are accuracy and thoroughness. Another type of report is one that must be submitted regularly and systematically. This type of report is known as the periodic report.

28. According to the passage above, accuracy and thoroughness are the *GREATEST* problems in the completion of 28.____

    A. one-page reports   B. form reports
    C. periodic reports   D. long reports

29. According to the passage above, a good written report from an operator to his supervisor should be 29.____

    A. printed
    B. formal
    C. periodic
    D. brief

Question 30.

DIRECTIONS: The sketches below show 150-lb. chlorine cylinders stored in three different ways:

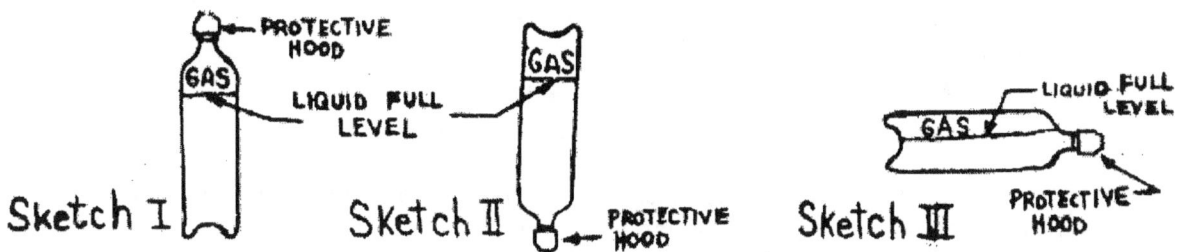

30. *Recommended* practice is to store a 150-lb. chlorine cylinder as shown in

    A. Sketch I *only*
    B. Sketch II *only*
    C. Sketch III *only*
    D. Sketches II and III

31. Of the following, the MOST serious defect in the installation shown below is that

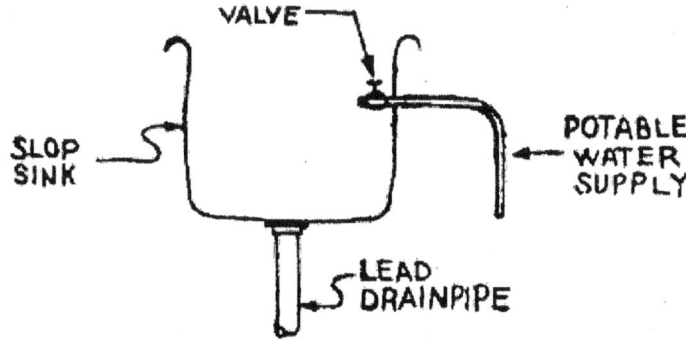

    A. the water supply should be directed downward to prevent excessive splashing over the rim
    B. the above installation may allow backflow of waste water into the water supply line
    C. lead pipes should not be used on drains from fixtures connected to the potable water supply
    D. excessive corrosion will occur on the valve if it becomes submerged

32. Of the following, the distance "x" which would be SAFEST when using the extension ladder shown in the sketch below is

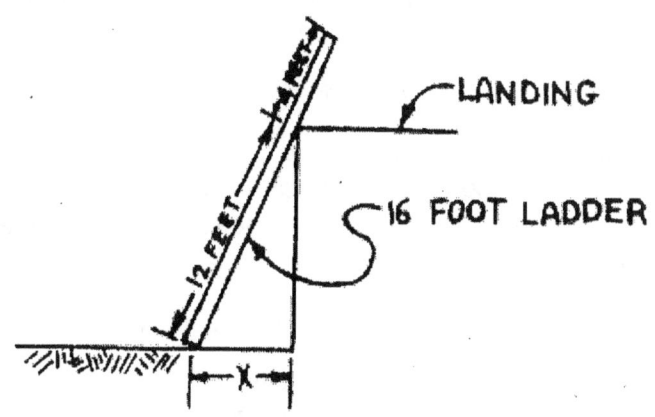

    A. 1 foot   B. 3 feet   C. 5 feet   D. 7 fee

33. Of the following statements regarding safe procedures for lifting a heavy object by yourself from the floor, the one which is FALSE is that

   A. you should keep your back as straight as possible
   B. you should bend your knees
   C. you should mainly use your back muscles in lifting
   D. your feet should be kept clear in case the object is dropped

34. It is generally not considered to be good practice to paint wood ladders. Of the following, the best reason for NOT painting wood ladders is that

   A. it may hide defects in the wood
   B. the rungs become slippery
   C. the hardware on the ladder becomes unworkable
   D. it would rub off on the surfaces against which it is resting

35. A rip saw would MOST likely be used to cut

   A. wood   B. steel   C. copper   D. aluminum

Questions 36-37.

DIRECTIONS: Questions 36 and 37 are to be answered SOLELY on the basis of the paragraph below.

NATURAL LAKES

Large lakes may yield water of exceptionally fine quality except near the shore line and in the vicinity of sewer outlets or near outlets of large streams. Therefore, minimum treatment is required. The availability of practically unlimited quantities of water is also a decided advantage. Unfortunately, however, the sewage from a city is often discharged into the same lake from which the water supply is taken. Great care must be taken in locating both the water intake and the sewer outlet so that the pollution handled by the water treatment plant is a minimum.

Sometimes the distance from the shore where dependable, satisfactory water can be found is so great that the cost of water intake facilities is prohibitive for a small municipality. In such cases, another supply must be found, or water must be obtained from a neighboring large city. Lake water is usually uniform in quality from day to day and does not vary in temperature as much as water from a river or small impounding reservoir.

36. A disadvantage of drawing a water supply from a large lake is that

   A. expensive treatment is required
   B. a limited quantity of water is available
   C. nearby cities may dump sewage into the lake
   D. the water is too cold.

37. An advantage of drawing a water supply from a large lake is that the

   A. water is uniform in quality
   B. water varies in temperature
   C. intake is distant from the shore
   D. intake may be near a sewer outlet

38. The *BEST* type of wrench to use to tighten a pipe without marring the pipe surface is   38.____

    A. pipe wrench
    B. strap wrench
    C. spanner wrench
    D. box wrench

39. Of the following statements concerning the use and care of files, the *one* which is *FALSE* is that   39.____

    A. files should have tight-fitting handles
    B. rasps are generally used on wood
    C. files should be protected by a light coating of oil when cutting metal
    D. files should be given a quick blow on a wood block to unclog teeth

40. A device which permits flow of a fluid in a pipe in one direction only is known as   40.____

    A. diode
    B. curb box
    C. gooseneck
    D. check valve

KEY (CORRECT ANSWERS)

1.	D	11.	B	21.	B	31.	B
2.	A	12.	A	22.	C	32.	B
3.	A	13.	A	23.	D	33.	C
4.	D	14.	D	24.	A	34.	A
5.	C	15.	C	25.	D	35.	A
6.	B	16.	D	26.	C	36.	C
7.	B	17.	A	27.	A	37.	A
8.	C	18.	D	28.	B	38.	B
9.	D	19.	D	29.	D	39.	C
10.	C	20.	A	30.	A	40.	D

TEST 2

DIRECTIONS: Each question or incomplete statement is followed by several suggested answers or completions. Select the one that *BEST* answers the question or completes the statement. *PRINT THE LETTER OF THE CORRECT ANSWER IN THE SPACE AT THE RIGHT.*

Questions 1-2.

DIRECTIONS: Questions 1 and 2 are to be answered *SOLELY* on the basis of the paragraph below.

PRECIPITATION AND RUNOFF

In the United States, the average annual precipitation is about 30 inches, of which about 21 inches is lost to the atmosphere by evaporation and transpiration. The remaining 9 inches becomes runoff into rivers and lakes. Both the precipitation and runoff vary greatly with geography and season. Annual precipitation varies from more than 100 inches in parts of the northwest to only 2 or 3 inches in parts of the southwest. In the northeastern part of the country, including New York State, the annual average precipitation is about 45 inches, of which about 22 inches becomes runoff. Even in New York State, there is some variation from place to place and considerable variation from time to time. During extremely dry years, the precipitation may be as low as 30 inches and the runoff below 10 inches. In general, there are greater variations in runoff rates from smaller watersheds. A critical water supply situation occurs when there are three or four abnormally dry years in succession.

Precipitation over the state is measured and recorded by a net-work of stations operated by the U. S. Weather Bureau. All of the precipitation records and other data such as temperature, humidity and evaporation rates are published monthly by the Weather Bureau in "Climatological Data." Runoff rates at more than 200 stream-gauging stations in the state are measured and recorded by the U. S. Geological Survey in cooperation with various state agencies. Records of the daily average flows are published annually by the U. S. Geological Survey in "Surface Water Records of New York." Copies may be obtained by writing to the Water Resources Division, United States Geological Survey, Albany, New York 23301.

1. From the above paragraphs it is *appropriate* to conclude that

   A. critical supply situations do not occur
   B. the greater the rainfall, the greater the runoff
   C. there are greater variations in runoff from larger watersheds
   D. the rainfall in the southwest is greater than the average in the country

2. From the above paragraphs, it is appropriate to conclude that

   A. an annual rainfall of about 50 inches does not occur in New York State
   B. the U. S. Weather Bureau is only interested in rainfall
   C. runoff is equal to rainfall less losses to the atmosphere
   D. information about rainfall and runoff in New York State is unavailable to the public

3. The following are diagrams of various types of bolt heads.

A B C D

The *one* of the above which is a Phillips head type is the one labelled
A. A   B. B   C. C   D. D

4. The appearance of frost on the outer surface of a chlorine cylinder which has been placed in service would *MOST* likely indicate that

A. the cylinder is empty
B. the gas is escaping too quickly from the cylinder
C. there is too much pressure in the cylinder
D. the humidity of the storage area is too high

5. One of the outer belts of a matched set of three V-belts becomes badly frayed. Of the following, the *BEST* course of action to take is to

A. replace only the worn belt
B. replace only the worn belt but put the new belt in the middle
C. remove the worn belt, put the center belt on the end and continue running the machine
D. replace the whole set of belts even if the other two belts show no signs of wear\

6. Of the following, the *BEST* type of valve to use for throttling or when the valve must be opened and closed frequently is a

A. check valve   B. globe valve
C. butterfly valve   D. pop valve

7. Of the following, the device which is used to measure *both* pressure and vacuum is the

A. compound gage   B. aquastat
C. pyrometer   D. thermocouple

8. Electrical energy is consumed and paid for in units of

A. voltage   B. ampere-hours
C. kilowatt-hours   D. watts

9. A "governor" on an engine is used to control the engine's

A. speed   B. temperature
C. interval of operation
D. engaging and disengaging the "load"

10. Pressure *below* that of the atmospheric pressure is usually expressed in

A. vacuum inches of mercury   B. inches of pressure absolute
C. BTU's   D. gallons per minute

11. A short piece of pipe with outside threads at both ends is called a 11.____

    A. union B. nipple C. tee D. sleeve

12. Of the following, which device would MOST likely produce water hammer in a plumbing installation? A(n) 12.____

    A. relief valve
    C. surge tank
    B. air chamber
    D. quick-closing valve

13. Some portable electric tools have a third conductor in the line cord which is electrically connected to the receptacle box. The reason for this is to 13.____

    A. have a spare wire in case one power wire breaks
    B. protect the user of the tool from electrical shock
    C. strengthen the power lead so that it cannot be easily damaged
    D. allow use of the tool for extended periods of time without overheating

14. Of the following, the device which is usually used to measure the rate of flow of water in a pipe is a 14.____

    A. pressure gage
    C. manometer
    B. Bourden gage
    D. velocity meter

15. Acid, rosin fluid, or paste applied to metal surfaces to remove oxide film in preparation for soldering is known as 15.____

    A. grout B. lampblack C. plumber's soil D. flux

16. In plumbing work, a coil spring which is inserted into a drain to facilitate cleaning of the drain is known as a 16.____

    A. pipe reamer B. snake C. plunger D. spigot

17. Of the following, a pneumatic device is one that is driven or powered by 17.____

    A. air pressure
    C. water pressure
    B. oil pressure
    D. steam pressure

18. Of the following metals, the one which would MOST likely be used for an electric motor shaft is 18.____

    A. wrought iron
    C. steel
    B. hard bronze
    D. bras

19. Of the following, a rotary gear pump is BEST suited for pumping 19.____

    A. #6 fuel oil B. hot water C. sewage D. kerosene

20. The MAIN reason for using a flexible coupling to join the shafts of two pieces of machinery together is that a flexible coupling 20.____

    A. allows for slight misalignment of the two shafts
    B. can be immediately disengaged in an emergency
    C. will automatically slip when overloaded thus protecting the driver machinery
    D. allows the driven load shaft to continue rotating under its own momentum, when the driver shaft is stopped

21. Of the following, the MAIN purpose of a house trap is to

    A. provide the house drain with a cleanout
    B. prevent gases from the public sewer from entering the house plumbing system
    C. trap articles of value that are accidentally dropped into the drainage pipes
    D. eliminate the necessity for traps under all other plumbing fixtures

22. Of the following, the MAIN reason for sometimes applying bituminous coating to the interiors of steel and cast-iron pipe is that this coating

    A. increases the tensile strength of the pipe
    B. increases the shock resistance of the pipe
    C. removes any objectionable taste from the water imparted by the pipe walls
    D. protects the pipe walls from corrosion

23. The one of the following electrical devices which is most likely to be used to raise or lower A.C. voltages is a

    A. resistor   B. thermistor   C. transformer   D. circuit-breaker

24. When a metal is galvanized, it is given a coating of

    A. nickel   B. tin   C. oxide   D. zinc

25. A conduit hickey is used to

    A. measure conduit pipe   B. bend conduit pipe
    C. thread conduit pipe   D. cut conduit pipe

Questions 26-27.

DIRECTIONS: Questions 26 and 27 are to be answered SOLELY on the basis of the electrical circuit shown below.

26. The circuit above is commonly known as a

    A. series circuit   B. parallel circuit
    C. short circuit   D. circuit breaker

27. The current flowing in the circuit above is

    A. 1 amp   B. 2 amps   C. 3 amps   D. 6 amps

Questions 28-30.

DIRECTIONS: Questions 28 to 30 inclusive are to be answered *SOLELY* on the basis of the sketches shown below.

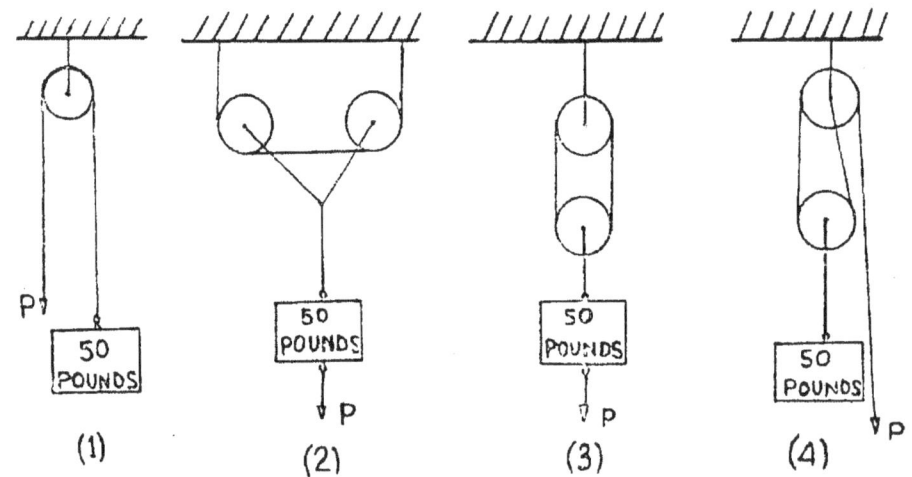

28. The two arrangements in the above diagrams which *CANNOT* be used to raise the load at all by applying a pull "p" as shown are setups

    A. 1 and 2   B. 2 and 3   C. 3 and 4   D. 1 and 4

29. The arrangement in the diagram above which requires the *LEAST* effort "p" to move the 50-pound weight is setup

    A. 1   B. 2   C. 3   D. 4

30. The effort required to hold the 50-pound weight at rest off the ground in setup (1) in the diagram above is

    A. 10 pounds   B. 25 pounds   C. 50 pounds   D. 100 pounds

31. Of the following formulas, the one which *CORRECTLY* shows the relationship between gage pressure and absolute pressure is

    A. Absolute pressure = gage pressure / atmospheric pressure
    B. Absolute pressure + gage pressure = atmospheric pressure
    C. Absolute pressure = gage pressure + atmospheric pressure
    D. Absolute pressure + atmospheric pressure = gage pressure

32. The weight of a gallon of water is, most nearly,

    A. 8.3 pounds   B. 16.6 pounds   C. 24.9 pounds   D. 33.2 pounds

33. Solenoid valves are usually operated

    A. thermally   B. manually   C. hydraulically   D. electrically

34. A 1/2-inch, 8-32 round-head machine screw has

    A. a diameter of 1/2 inch
    B. a length of 8 inches
    C. 8 threads per inch
    D. 32 threads per inch

35. The MAIN purpose for the stuffing usually found in centrifugal pump stuffing boxes is

    A. supporting the shaft
    B. controlling the rate of discharge
    C. preventing fluid leakage
    D. compensating for shaft misalignment

36. The BEST wrench to use on screwed valves and fittings having hexagonal shape connections is the

    A. chain wrench
    B. open-end wrench
    C. pipe wrench
    D. strap wrench

37. A tap is a tool commonly used to

    A. remove broken screws
    B. flare pipe ends
    C. cut external threads
    D. cut internal threads

38. A thread chaser is MOST likely to be used to

    A. rethread damaged threads
    B. remove broken taps
    C. flare tubing
    D. adjust diestocks

39. If an air-conditioning unit shorted out and caught fire, the BEST fire extinguisher to use would be a

    A. water extinguisher
    B. foam extinguisher
    C. carbon dioxide extinguisher
    D. soda acid extinguisher

40. Of the following, the best action to take to help someone whose eyes have been splashed with lye is to FIRST

    A. wash out the eyes with clean water
    B. wash out the eyes with a salt water solution
    C. apply a sterile dressing over the eyes
    D. do nothing to the eyes, but telephone for medical help

KEY (CORRECT ANSWERS)

1. B	11. B	21. B	31. C
2. C	12. D	22. D	32. A
3. C	13. B	23. C	33. D
4. B	14. D	24. D	34. D
5. D	15. D	25. B	35. C
6. B	16. B	26. A	36. B
7. A	17. A	27. B	37. D
8. C	18. C	28. B	38. A
9. A	19. A	29. D	39. C
10. A	20. A	30. C	40. A

SAFETY
EXAMINATION SECTION
TEST 1

DIRECTIONS: Each question or incomplete statement is followed by several suggested answers or completions. Select the one that BEST answers the question or completes the statement. *PRINT THE LETTER OF THE CORRECT ANSWER IN THE SPACE AT THE RIGHT.*

1. There are two indicators used to determine the safety record of an agency. One is the "frequency of injury," and the other is the "severity of injury."
   The "frequency of injury" is considered a better indicator of the safety record because

   A. blind chance has a greater effect on "severity" than on "frequency"
   B. it is easier to record "frequency" than "severity"
   C. workers will pay more attention to "frequency" than to "severity"
   D. it is more difficult to determine the "severity" than the "frequency"

   1.____

2. It is frequently said that some people are "accident prone." This term should be applied ONLY to those people who

   A. fail to respond to safety training
   B. have accidents when the cause of the accident cannot be determined
   C. lack the physical capacity for their job
   D. do not have the skill required to do a certain job

   2.____

3. "Accidents frequently happen because a man *daydreams* on the job." Of the following, the one that is CORRECT based on the previous sentence is:

   A. Accidents are most often caused by *daydreaming*
   B. The main cause of poor work is accidents
   C. A man who does not *daydream* is a good worker
   D. It is important for a man to pay attention to what he is doing

   3.____

4. Accidents can be classified as caused either by "unsafe acts" or "unsafe conditions." The one of the following that would be considered as "unsafe condition'" is

   A. jumping over an obstruction on the floor
   B. poor lighting in a crowded cellar
   C. speeding in a motor vehicle
   D. use of the wrong tool for a job

   4.____

5. Of the following types of fires, a soda-acid fire extinguisher is NOT recommended for

   A. electric motor controls   B. waste paper
   C. waste rags   D. wood desks

   5.____

6. A foam-type fire extinguisher extinguishes fires by

   A. cooling only   B. drenching only
   C. smothering only   D. cooling and smothering

   6.____

55

7. If an air-conditioning unit shorted out and caught fire, the BEST fire extinguisher to use would be _____ extinguisher.

    A. water
    B. foam
    C. carbon dioxide
    D. soda acid

8. The one of the following diseases which may be caused by the pollution of drinking water by sewage is

    A. malaria
    B. typhoid fever
    C. tuberculosis
    D. muscular dystrophy

9. The type of portable fire extinguisher that is MOST effective in controlling a fire around live electrical equipment is the

    A. foam type
    B. soda-acid type
    C. carbon-dioxide type
    D. water type

10. The hazards of electric shock resulting from operation of a portable electric tool in a damp location can be *reduced* by

    A. grounding the tool
    B. holding the tool with one hand
    C. running the tool at low speed
    D. using a baffle

11. The MAIN reason caretakers are advised to always wear protective goggles while changing a broken bulb is to avoid the danger of

    A. glare from the bulb
    B. pieces of glass getting in the eyes
    C. sparks from the bulb
    D. insects on or around the bulb socket

12. Of the following types of fire extinguishers, the one to use on an electrical fire is

    A. soda acid
    B. carbon dioxide
    C. water pump tank
    D. pyrene

13. The GREATEST number of injuries from equipment used in construction work result from

    A. carelessness of the operator
    B. poor maintenance of the equipment
    C. overloading of the equipment
    D. poor inspection of the equipment

14. Of the following, the BEST way a laborer can avoid accidents is to

    A. work slowly
    B. be alert
    C. wear safety shoes
    D. wear glasses

15. Of the following actions, the BEST one to take FIRST after smoke is seen coming from an electric control device is to

    A. shut off the power to it
    B. call the main office for advice
    C. look for a wiring diagram
    D. throw water on it

16. Of the following fire extinguishers, the one which should be provided for use in the elevator machine room is the

    A. carbon-dioxide type
    B. soda-acid type
    C. foam type
    D. loaded-stream type

17. Frequent deaths are reported as a result of running an automobile engine in a closed garage. Death results from

    A. suffocation
    B. carbon monoxide poisoning
    C. excessive humidity
    D. an excess of carbon dioxide in the air

18. As a veteran sewage treatment worker, you can BEST promote safety in your operations by

    A. carefully investigating and reporting the circumstances of any accident
    B. suggesting safer methods of operation
    C. training subordinates in proper safety
    D. disciplining subordinates who engage in unsafe acts

19. Oil soaked rags are BEST stored in a

    A. neat pile in a readily accessible corner
    B. metal container with a tight cover
    C. metal box that has holes for adequate ventilation
    D. closet on a shelf above the ground

20. The one of the following actions that is NOT the cause of injury when working with hand tools is

    A. working with defective tools
    B. using the wrong tool for the job
    C. working too carefully
    D. using a tool improperly

21. To safely lift a heavy object from the ground, you should keep your arms and elbows

    A. away from the body with your back bent
    B. away from the body with your back straight
    C. close to the body with your back bent
    D. close to the body with your back straight

Questions 22-25.

DIRECTIONS: Each question consists of a statement. You are to indicate whether the statement is TRUE (T) or FALSE (F). *PRINT THE LETTER OF THE CORRECT ANSWER IN THE SPACE AT THE RIGHT.*

22. The foam type extinguisher is not suitable for use on gasoline fires. 22.____

23. The first thing an employee should do when he sees a smoking electric wire is to throw water on the wire. 23.____

24. Many accidents are caused by carelessness of employees while at work. 24.____

25. If, at work, you are unable to lift a very heavy object, you should rest a couple of minutes and try again. 25.____

KEY (CORRECT ANSWERS)

1.	A	11.	B
2.	A	12.	B
3.	D	13.	A
4.	B	14.	B
5.	A	15.	A
6.	D	16.	A
7.	C	17.	B
8.	B	18.	C
9.	C	19.	B
10.	A	20.	C

21. D
22. F
23. F
24. T
25. F

TEST 2

DIRECTIONS: Each question or incomplete statement is followed by several suggested answers or completions. Select the one that BEST answers the question or completes the statement. *PRINT THE LETTER OF THE CORRECT ANSWER IN THE SPACE AT THE RIGHT.*

1. Assume that a fire breaks out in an electrical control panel board. Of the following types of portable fire extinguishers, the BEST one to use to put out this fire would be a   1.____
   - A. dry-chemical type
   - B. soda-acid type
   - C. foam type
   - D. water-stream type

2. The MAJORITY of home accidents result from   2.____
   - A. burns
   - B. suffocation
   - C. falls
   - D. poisons

3. A soda-acid fire extinguisher is recommended for use on fires consisting of   3.____
   - A. wood or paper
   - B. fuel oil or gasoline
   - C. electrical causes or fuel oil
   - D. paint or turpentine

4. Of the following, the extinguishing agent that should be used on fires in flammable liquids is   4.____
   - A. steam
   - B. water
   - C. foam
   - D. soda and acid

5. Of the following, the BEST way to put out a gasoline fire is to use   5.____
   - A. a carbon dioxide extinguisher
   - B. compressed air
   - C. water
   - D. rags to smother the blaze

6. A heavy object should be lifted by first crouching and firmly grasping the object to be lifted. Then, the worker should lift   6.____
   - A. using his back muscles and keeping his legs bent
   - B. by straightening his legs and keeping his back as straight as possible
   - C. using his arm muscles and keeping his back nearly horizontal
   - D. using his arm muscles and keeping his feet close together

7. The proper type of firefighting equipment to be used on an electrical fire is a   7.____
   - A. soda-acid type extinguisher
   - B. fire hose and water
   - C. dry-chemical type extinguisher
   - D. foam type extinguisher

8. While working on the job, you accidentally break a window pane. No one is around, and you are able to clean up the broken pieces of glass. It would then be BEST for you to

   A. leave a note near the window that a new glass has to be put in because it was accidentally broken
   B. forget about the whole thing because the window was not broken on purpose
   C. write a report to your supervisor telling him that you saw a broken window pane that has to be fixed
   D. tell your supervisor that you accidentally broke the window pane while working

8._____

9. The BEST way to remove some small pieces of broken glass from a floor is to

   A. use a brush and dust pan
   B. pick up the pieces carefully with your hands
   C. use a wet mop and a wringer
   D. sweep the pieces into the corner of the room

9._____

10. Employees should wipe up water spilled on floors immediately. The BEST reason for this is that water on a floor

    A. is a sign that employees are sloppy
    B. makes for a slippery condition that could cause an accident
    C. will eat into the wax protecting the floor
    D. is against health regulations

10._____

11. A carbon dioxide fire extinguisher is BEST suited for extinguishing

    A. paper fires   B. rag fires
    C. rubbish fires   D. grease fires

11._____

12. A pressurized water or soda-acid fire extinguisher is BEST suited for extinguishing

    A. wood fires   B. gasoline fires
    C. electrical fires   D. magnesium fires

12._____

13. Assume that an officer, alone in a building at night, smells the strong odor of cooking or heating gas. In addition to airing the building and making sure that he is not overcome, it would be BEST for the officer to call

    A. his superior at his home and ask for instructions
    B. for a plumber from the department of public works
    C. 911 for police and fire help
    D. the emergency number at Con Edison

13._____

14. The one of the following which is the MOST common safety hazard in an office is

    A. a sharp pencil on a desk
    B. an open desk drawer
    C. lack of covers for electric computers
    D. lack of parallel alignment of desks

14._____

15. Which of the following situations is MOST likely to pose the greatest danger to safety?

    A. Buffing a main corridor to a high shine
    B. Leaving a door to a hall open at a 180 angle

15._____

C. Opening the top two drawers of a four-drawer file cabinet
D. Setting a desk at a 45 angle near a main aisle in an office

16. Safety experts agree that accidents can probably BEST be prevented by

    A. developing safety consciousness among employees
    B. developing a program which publicizes major accidents
    C. penalizing employees the first time they do not follow safety procedures
    D. giving recognition to employees with accident-free records

17. The accident records of many agencies indicate that most on-the-job injuries are caused by the unsafe acts of their employees. Which one of the following statements pinpoints the *most probable* cause of this safety problem?

    A. Responsibility for preventing on-the-job accidents has not been delegated.
    B. Lack of proper supervision has permitted these unsafe actions to continue.
    C. No consideration has been given to eliminating environmental job hazards.
    D. Penalties for causing on-the-job accidents are not sufficiently severe.

18. Which of the following methods is LEAST essential to the success of an accident prevention program?

    A. Determining corrective measures by analyzing the causes of accidents and making recommendations to eliminate them
    B. Educating employees as to the importance of safe working conditions and methods
    C. Determining accident causes by seeking out the conditions from which each accident has developed
    D. Holding each supervisor responsible for accidents occurring during the on-the-job performance of his immediate subordinates

19. Assume that you have a bad cold and take a strong decongestant pill before you come to work. You are scheduled, that day, to drive an official car to a supermarket to make an inspection. Of the following, it would be BEST for you to

    A. drive to the store and make the inspection as usual
    B. drive to the store very slowly and carefully, since you are not feeling well
    C. explain to your supervisor that you should not drive that day
    D. start out to make the inspection, but return to the office if you feel your driving ability is impaired

20. Of the following office supplies, the kind which you should usually be MOST careful to keep away from an open flame is

    A. carbon paper   B. ink
    C. paste   D. typing paper

21. The only one of the following types of fire extinguishers which should generally NOT be used to extinguish a gasoline fire is

    A. carbon dioxide   B. dry chemical
    C. foam   D. water

Questions 22-25.

DIRECTIONS: Each question consists of a statement. You are to indicate whether the statement is TRUE (T) or FALSE (F). *PRINT THE LETTER OF THE CORRECT ANSWER IN THE SPACE AT THE RIGHT.*

22. In directing the stream from a foam-type extinguisher at a fire, the extinguisher should be held upside down. 22.____

23. The carbon tetrachloride type of extinguisher is the most effective for use on electrical fires. 23.____

24. A soda-and-acid type of extinguisher should be refilled at least once in five years. 24.____

25. In lifting heavy articles, sanitation men should keep their feet wide apart. 25.____

KEY (CORRECT ANSWERS)

1.	A	11.	D
2.	C	12.	A
3.	A	13.	D
4.	C	14.	B
5.	A	15.	C
6.	B	16.	A
7.	C	17.	B
8.	D	18.	D
9.	A	19.	C
10.	B	20.	A

21. D
22. T
23. T
24. F
25. F

MECHANICAL APTITUDE
TOOL RECOGNITION AND USE
EXAMINATION SECTION
TEST 1

DIRECTIONS: Each question or incomplete statement is followed by several suggested answers or completions. Select the one that BEST answers the question or completes the statement. *PRINT THE LETTER OF THE CORRECT ANSWER IN THE SPACE AT THE RIGHT.*

Questions 1-16.

DIRECTIONS: Questions 1 through 16 refer to the tools shown below. The numbers in the answers refer to the numbers below the tools. NOTE: These tools are NOT shown to scale.

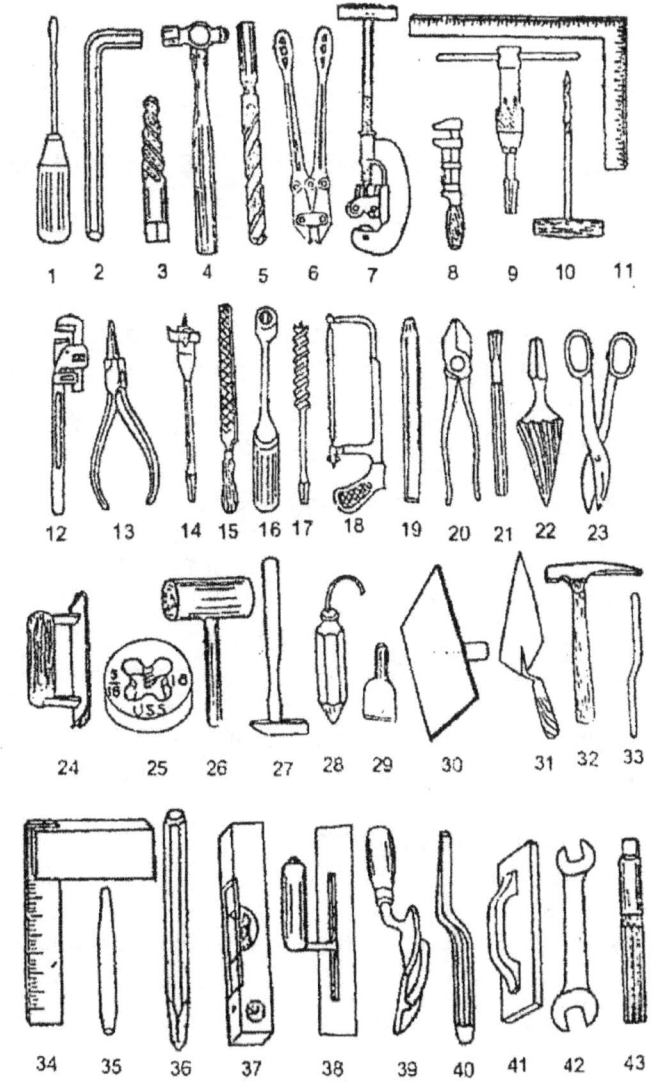

2 (#1)

1. In order to cut a piece of 5/16" diameter steel scaffold hoisting cable, you should use tool number
   A. 6   B. 7   C. 19   D. 23

   1._____

2. Scaffold planks are secured to joisting irons by means of lag screws.
   To properly tighten these lag screws, you should use tool number
   A. 12   B. 13   C. 20   D. 42

   2._____

3. While installing a steel angle iron lintel, you find that the threads on the embedded holding bolts are damaged.
   You should repair the threads by using tool number
   A. 7   B. 9   C. 25   D. 43

   3._____

4. It is necessary to cut a hole in a concrete foundation wall in order to place a small bolt.
   To cut this small hole, you should use tool number
   A. 14   B. 19   C. 21   D. 40

   4._____

5. If tool number 17 bears the mark "7," this tool should be used to drill holes having a diameter of
   A. 7/64"   B. 7/32"   C. 7/16"   D. 7/8"

   5._____

6. If the marking on the blade of tool number 18 reads "10-18," the "18" refers to the
   A. number of teeth per inch   B. weight
   C. thickness   D. length

   6._____

7. If two points are separated by a vertical distance of 12 feet, the tool that should be used to make certain that the points are in perfect vertical alignment is number
   A. 11   B. 28   C. 34   D. 37

   7._____

8. A 3/4" diameter hole must be made in a steel floor beam.
   The tool you should use is number
   A. 3   B. 5   C. 9   D. 22

   8._____

9. To cut the corner off a building brick, you should use tool number
   A. 4   B. 27   C. 29   D. 36

   9._____

10. A 2" x 2" x 3/16" steel angle should be cut using tool number
    A. 6   B. 7   C. 18   D. 19

    10._____

11. The term "snips" should be applied to tool number
    A. 6   B. 13   C. 20   D. 23

    11._____

12. To line-up the bolt holes in two structural steel beams, you should use tool number
    A. 1   B. 33   C. 35   D. 36

    12._____

13. A "hawk" is tool number 13.____
    A. 29 B. 30 C. 38 D. 41

14. After an 8" thick brick wall has been erected, it is discovered that a hole 14.____
    should have been left for a 4" sewer pipe.
    To cut that hole, you should use tool number
    A. 5 B. 19 C. 32 D. 36

15. A "float" is tool number 15.____
    A. 30 B. 31 C. 33 D. 41

16. A "Stillson" is tool number 16.____
    A. 2 B. 8 C. 12 D. 22

KEY (CORRECT ANSWERS)

1.	A	11.	D
2.	D	12.	C
3.	C	13.	B
4.	C	14.	D
5.	C	15.	D
6.	A	16.	C
7.	B		
8.	B		
9.	C		
10.	C		

TEST 2

DIRECTIONS: Each question or incomplete statement is followed by several suggested answers or completions. Select the one that BEST answers the question or completes the statement. *PRINT THE LETTER OF THE CORRECT ANSWER IN THE SPACE AT THE RIGHT.*

1. The stake shown in the sketch at the right is a _____ stake.
    A. hatchet
    B. conductor
    C. solid mandrel
    D. beak horn

    1._____

2. When a circle is too large to be drawn with a pair of dividers, the PROPER tool to use is a
    A. trammel
    B. protractor
    C. combination set
    D. flexible curve

    2._____

3. A rivet set is a tool used to
    A. shape the head of a rivet
    B. mark off the spacing of rivets
    C. remove a loose rivet
    D. check the shank length of a rivet

    3._____

4. The hammer shown in the sketch at the right is a _____ hammer.
    A. raising
    B. ball peen
    C. setting
    D. cross-over

    4._____

5. Of the following, the BEST tool to use to scribe a line parallel to the straight edge of a piece of sheet metal is a(n)
    A. outside caliper
    B. pair of dividers
    C. template
    D. scratch gage

    5._____

6. Of the following, the BEST device to use to check the condition of the insulation of a cable is the
    A. ohmmeter
    B. wheatstone bridge
    C. voltmeter
    D. megger

    6._____

7. Of the following fittings, the one used to connect two lengths of conduit in a straight line is a(n)
    A. elbow
    B. nipple
    C. tee
    D. coupling

    7._____

8. If a nut is to be tightened to an exact specified value, the wrench that should be used is a(n) _____ wrench.
    A. torque
    B. lock-jaw
    C. alligator
    D. spaner

    8._____

9. A stillson wrench is also called a _____ wrench.
   A. strap   B. pipe   C. monkey   D. crescent

10. A machine screw is indicated on a drawing as. The head is the American Standard type called
    A. flat
    B. oval
    C. fillister
    D. round

11. The tool that is shown at the right is properly referred to as a(n) _____ tap.
    A. bottoming
    B. acme
    C. taper
    D. plug

12. The tool indicated at the right is referred to as an Arc Punch. This tool should be used to
    A. cut holes in 1/16" steel
    B. cut large diameter holes in masonry
    C. run through a conduit prior to pulling a cable or wires
    D. make holes in rubber or leather gasket material

13. The plumbing fitting shown at the right is called a
    A. street elbow
    B. return bend
    C. running trap
    D. reversing "el"

14. For which one of the following uses would it be unsafe to use a carpenter's hammer?
    A. casing mail   B. hand punch
    C. hardened steel surface   D. plastic surface

15. Of the following, the MAIN advantage in using a Phillips head screw is that
    A. the threads of the Phillips head screw have a deeper bite than standard screw threads
    B. the screwdriver used on this type of screw is more likely to keep its edge than a standard screwdriver
    C. a single screwdriver fits all size screws of this type
    D. the screwdriver used on this type of screw is less likely to slip than a standard screwdriver

16. One of the reasons why a polyester rope is considered to be the BEST general purpose rope is that it
    A. does not stretch as much as ropes made of other materials
    B. is available in longer lengths than ropes made of other materials
    C. does not fray as much as ropes made of other materials
    D. contains more strands than ropes made of other materials

17. The PROPER saw to use to cut wood with the grain is a _____ saw.
    A. hack   B. crosscut   C. back   D. rip

18. Assume that the instruction manual for a machine indicates that a certain bolt must be tightened with a specified amount of force.
    Of the following tools, the one which should be used to tighten the bolt with the specified amount of force is a(n) _____ wrench.
    A. torque   B. adjustable   C. stillson   D combination

19. The power source of a pneumatic tool is
    A. manual
    B. water pressure
    C. compressed air
    D. electricity

20. The tool used to cut internal pipe threads is a
    A. broach   B. tap   C. die   D. rod

KEY (CORRECT ANSWERS)

1.	A	11.	A
2.	A	12.	D
3.	A	13.	B
4.	C	14.	C
5.	D	15.	D
6.	D	16.	A
7.	D	17.	D
8.	A	18.	A
9.	B	19.	C
10.	B	20.	B

MECHANICAL APTITUDE TOOLS AND THEIR USE

EXAMINATION SECTION
TEST 1

Questions 1-16.

DIRECTIONS: Questions 1 through 16 refer to the tools shown below. The numbers in the answers refer to the numbers beneath the tools.
NOTE: These tools are NOT shown to scale

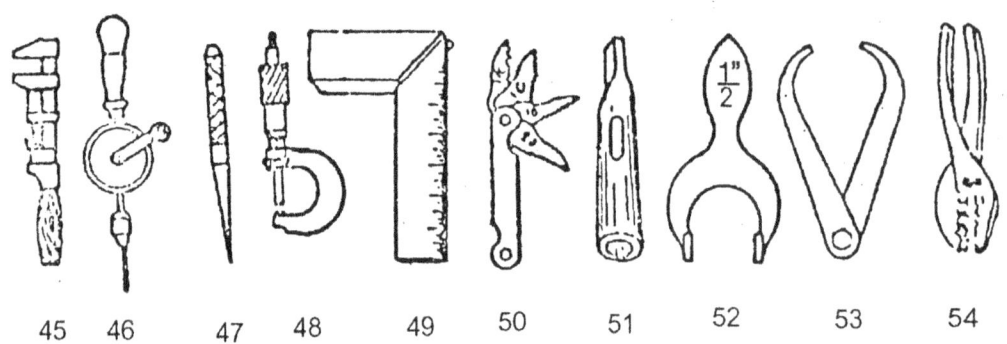

45 46 47 48 49 50 51 52 53 54

1. A 1" x 1" x 1/8" angle iron should be cut by using tool number
   A. 7   B. 12   C. 23   D. 42

2. To peen an iron rivet, you should use tool number
   A. 4   B. 7   C. 21   D. 43

3. The star "drill" is tool number
   A. 5   B. 10   C. 20   D. 22

4. To make holes in sheet metal for sheet metal screws, you should use tool number.
   A. 6   B. 10   C. 36   D. 46

5. To cut through a 3/8" diameter wire rope, you should use tool number
   A. 12   B. 23   C. 42   D. 54

6. To remove cutting burrs from the inside of a steel pipe, you should use tool number
   A. 5   B. 11   C. 14   D. 20

7. The depth of a bored hole may be measured MOST accurately with tool number
   A. 8   B. 16   C. 26   D. 41

8. If the marking on the blade of tool number 7 reads:12"-32", the 32 refers to the
   A. length   B. thickness   C. weight
   D. number of teeth per inch

9. If tool number 6 bears the mark "5", it should be used to drill holes having a diameter of
   A. 5/32"   B. 5/16"   C. 5/8"   D. 5"

10. To determine MOST quickly the number of threads per inch on a bolt, you should use tool number
    A. 8   B. 16   C. 26   D. 50

11. Wood screws, located in positions where the headroom does not permit the use of an ordinary screwdriver, may be removed by using tool number
    A. 17   B. 28   C. 35   D. 46

12. To remove a broken-off piece of 1/2" diameter pipe from a fitting, you should use tool number

   A. 5   B. 11   C. 20   D. 36

13. The outside diameter of a bushing may be measured MOST accurately with tool number

   A. 8   B. 26   C. 33   D. 43

14. To re-thread a stud hole in the casting of an elevator motor, you should use tool number

   A. 5   B. 20   C. 22   D. 36

15. To enlarge slightly a bored hole in a steel plate, you should use tool number

   A. 5   B. 11   C. 20   D. 36

16. The term "16 oz." should be applied to tool number

   A. 1   B. 12   C. 21   D. 42

KEYS (CORRECT ANSWERS)

1. A
2. C
3. B
4. D
5. B
6. B
7. B
8. D
9. B
10. D
11. C
12. C
13. C
14. D
15. A
16. C

TEST 2

Questions 1-11.

DIRECTIONS: Questions 1 through 11 refer to the instruments listed below. Each instrument is listed with an identifying number in front of it.

   1 - Hygrometer
   2 - Ammeter
   3 - Voltmeter
   4 - Wattmeter
   5 - Megger
   6 - Oscilloscope
   7 - Frequency meter
   8 - Micrometer
   9 - Vernier calliper
   10 - Wire gage
   11 - 6-foot folding rule
   12 - Architect's scale
   13 - Planimeter
   14 - Engineer's scale
   15 - Ohmmeter

1. The instrument that should be used to *accurately* measure the resistance of a 4,700-ohm resistor is number

   A. 3   B. 4   C. 7   D. 15

2. To measure the current in an electrical circuit, the instrument that should be used is number

   A. 2   B. 7   C. 8   D. 15

3. To measure the insulation resistance of a rubber-covered electrical cable, the instrument that should be used is number

   A. 4   B. 5   C. 8   D. 15

4. An AC motor is hooked up to a power distribution box. In order to check the voltage at the motor terminals, the instrument that should be used is number

   A. 2   B. 3   C. 4   D. 7

5. To measure the shaft diameter of a motor *accurately* to one-thousandth of an inch, the instrument that should be used is number

   A. 8   B. 10   C. 11   D. 14

6. The instrument that should be used to determine whether 25 Hz. or 60 Hz. is present in an electrical circuit is number

   A. 4   B. 5   C. 7   D. 8

7. Of the following, the *proper* instrument to use to determine the diameter of the conductor of a piece of electrical hookup wire is number

   A. 10   B. 11   C. 12   D. 14

8. The amount of electrical power being used in a balanced three-phase circuit should be measured with number

   A. 2   B. 3   C. 4   D. 5

9. The electrical wave form at a given point in an electronic circuit can be observed with number

   A. 2   B. 3   C. 6   D. 7

10. The *proper* instrument to use for measuring the width of a door is number   10.____

    A. 11   B. 12   C. 13   D. 14

11. A one-inch hole with a tolerance of plus or minus three-thousandths is reamed in a steel   11.____
    block. The *proper* instrument to accurately check the diameter of the hole is number

    A. 8   B. 9   C. 11   D. 14

12. An oilstone is LEAST likely to be used correctly to sharpen a   12.____

    A. scraper   B. chisel   C. knife   D. saw

13. To cut the ends of a number of lengths of wood at an angle of 45 degrees, it would be   13.____
    BEST to use a

    A. mitre-box   B. protractor   C. triangle   D. wooden rule

14. A gouge is a tool used for   14.____

    A. planing wood smooth   B. grinding metal
    C. drilling steel   D. chiseling wood

15. Holes are usually countersunk when installing   15.____

    A. carriage bolts   B. lag screws
    C. flat-head screws   D. square nuts

16. A tool that is *generally* used to slightly elongate a round hole in scrap-iron is a   16.____

    A. rat-tail file   B. reamer   C. drill   D. rasp

17. When the term "10-24" is used to specify a machine screw, the number 24 refers to the   17.____

    A. number of screws per pound   B. diameter of the screw
    C. length of the screw   D. number of threads per inch

18. If you were unable to tighten a nut by means of a ratchet wrench because, although the   18.____
    nut turned on with the forward movement of the wrench, it turned off with the backward
    movement, you should

    A. make the nut hand-tight before using the wrench
    B. reverse the ratchet action
    C. put a few drops of oil on the wrench
    D. use a different socket in the handle

19. If you were installing a long wood screw and found you were unable to drive this screw   19.____
    more than three-quarters of its length by the use of a properly-fitting straight-handled
    screwdriver, the *proper* SUBSEQUENT action would be for you to

    A. take out the screw and put soap on it
    B. change to the use of a screwdriver-bit and brace
    C. take out the screw and drill a shorter hole before redriving
    D. use a pair of pliers on the blade of the screwdriver

20. Good practice requres that the end of a pipe to be installed in a plumbing system be reamed to remove the inside burr after it has been cut to length. The *purpose* of this reaming is to

   A. restore the original inside diameter of the pipe at the end
   B. remove loose rust
   C. make the threading of the pipe easier
   D. finish the pipe accurately to length

20.____

KEYS (CORRECT ANSWERS)

1.	D	11.	B
2.	A	12.	D
3.	B	13.	A
4.	B	14.	D
5.	A	15.	C
6.	C	16.	A
7.	A	17.	D
8.	C	18.	A
9.	C	19.	A
10.	A	20.	A

EXAMINATION SECTION
TEST 1

DIRECTIONS: Each question or incomplete statement is followed by several suggested answers or completions. Select the one that BEST answers the question or completes the statement. *PRINT THE LETTER OF THE CORRECT ANSWER IN THE SPACE AT THE RIGHT.*

1. In public agencies, communications should be based PRIMARILY on a
   A. two-way flow from the top down and from the bottom up, most of which should be given in writing to avoid ambiguity
   B. multi-direction flow among all levels and with outside persons
   C. rapid, internal one-way flow from the top down
   D. two-way flow of information, most of which should be given orally for purposes of clarity

2. In some organizations, changes in policy or procedures are often communicated by word of mouth from supervisors to employees with no prior discussion or exchange of viewpoints with employees.
   This procedure often produces employee dissatisfaction CHIEFLY because
   A. information is mostly unusable since a considerable amount of time is required to transmit information
   B. lower-level supervisors tend to be excessively concerned with minor details
   C. management has failed to seek employees' advice before making changes
   D. valuable staff time is lost between decision-making and the implementation of decisions

3. For good letter writing, you should try to visualize the person to whom you are writing, especially if you know him.
   Of the following rules, it is LEAST helpful in such visualization to think of
   A. the person's likes and dislikes, his concerns, and his needs
   B. what you would be likely to say if speaking in person
   C. what you would expect to be asked if speaking in person
   D. your official position in order to be certain that your words are proper

4. One approach to good informal letter writing is to make letters and conversational.
   All of the following practices will usually help to do this EXCEPT:
   A. If possible, use a style which is similar to the style used when speaking
   B. Substitute phrases for single words (e.g., *at the present time* for *now*)
   C. Use contractions of words (e.g., *you're* for *you are*)
   D. Use ordinary vocabulary when possible

5. All of the following rules will aid in producing clarity in report-writing EXCEPT:
   A. Give specific details or examples, if possible
   B. Keep related words close together in each sentence
   C. Present information in sequential order
   D. Put several thoughts or ideas in each paragraph

6. The one of the following statements about public relations which is MOST accurate is that
   A. in the long run, appearance gains better results than performance
   B. objectivity is decreased if outside public relations consultants are employed
   C. public relations is the responsibility of every employee
   D. public relations should be based on a formal publicity program

7. The form of communication which is usually considered to be MOST personally directed to the intended recipient is the
   A. brochure   B. film   C. letter   D. radio

8. In general, a document that presents an organization's views or opinions on a particular topic is MOST accurately known as a
   A. tear sheet   B. position paper
   C. flyer   D. journal

9. Assume that you have been asked to speak before an organization of persons who oppose a newly announced program in which you are involved. You feel tense about talking to this group.
   Which of the following rules generally would be MOST useful in gaining rapport when speaking before the audience?
   A. Impress them with your experience
   B. Stress all areas of disagreement
   C. Talk to the group as to one person
   D. Use formal grammar and language

10. An organization must have an effective public relations program since, at its best, public relations is a bridge to change.
    All of the following statements about communication and human behavior have validity EXCEPT:
    A. People are more likely to talk about controversial matters with like-minded people than with those holding other views
    B. The earlier an experience, the more powerful its effect since it influences how later experiences will be interpreted
    C. In periods of social tension, official sources gain increased believability
    D. Those who are already interested in a topic are the ones who are most open to receive new communications about it

11. An employee should be encouraged to talk easily and frankly when he is dealing with his supervisor.
    In order to encourage such free communication, it would be MOST appropriate for a supervisor to behave in a(n)
    A. sincere manner; assure the employee that you will deal with him honestly and openly
    B. official manner; you are a supervisor and must always act formally with subordinates
    C. investigative manner; you must probe and question to get to a basis of trust
    D. unemotional manner; the employee's emotions and background should play no part in your dealings with him

11._____

12. Research findings show that an increase in free communication within an agency GENERALLY results in which one of the following?
    A. Improved morale and productivity
    B. Increased promotional opportunities
    C. An increase in authority
    D. A spirit of honesty

12._____

13. Assume that you are a supervisor and your superiors have given you a new-type procedure to be followed.
    Before passing this information on to your subordinates, the one of the following actions that you should take FIRST is to
    A. ask your superiors to send out a memorandum to the entire staff
    B. clarify the procedure in your own mind
    C. set up a training course to provide instruction on the new procedure
    D. write a memorandum to your subordinates

13._____

14. Communication is necessary for an organization to be effective.
    The one of the following which is LEAST important for most communication systems is that
    A. messages are sent quickly and directly to the person who needs them to operate
    B. information should be conveyed understandably and accurately
    C. the method used to transmit information should be kept secret so that security can be maintained
    D. senders of messages must know how their messages are received and acted upon

14._____

15. Which one of the following is the CHIEF advantage of listening willingly to subordinates and encouraging them to talk freely and honestly?
    It
    A. reveals to supervisors the degree to which ideas that are passed down are accepted by subordinates
    B. reduces the participation of subordinates in the operation of the department
    C. encourages subordinates to try for promotion
    D. enables supervisors to learn more readily what the *grapevine* is saying

15._____

16. A supervisor may be informed through either oral or written reports. 16.____
Which one of the following is an ADVANTAGE of using oral reports?
   A. There is no need for a formal record of the report.
   B. An exact duplicate of the report is not easily transmitted to others.
   C. A good oral report requires little time for preparation.
   D. An oral report involves two-way communication between a subordinate and his supervisor.

17. Of the following, the MOST important reason why supervisors should 17.____
communicate effectively with the public is to
   A. improve the public's understanding of information that is important for them to know
   B. establish a friendly relationship
   C. obtain information about the kinds of people who come to the agency
   D. convince the public that services are adequate

18. Supervisors should generally NOT use phrases like *too hard*, *too easy*, and 18.____
a lot PRINCIPALLY because such phrases
   A. may be offensive to some minority groups
   B. are too informal
   C. mean different things to different people
   D. are difficult to remember

19. The ability to communicate clearly and concisely is an important element in 19.____
effective leadership.
Which of the following statements about oral and written communication is GENERALLY true?
   A. Oral communication is more time-consuming.
   B. Written communication is more likely to be misinterpreted.
   C. Oral communication is useful only in emergencies.
   D. Written communication is useful mainly when giving information to fewer than twenty people.

20. Rumors can often have harmful and disruptive effects on an organization. 20.____
Which one of the following is the BEST way to prevent rumors from becoming a problem?
   A. Refuse to act on rumors, thereby making them less believable.
   B. Increase the amount of information passed along by the *grapevine*.
   C. Distribute as much factual information as possible.
   D. Provide training in report writing.

21. Suppose that a subordinate asks you about a rumor he has heard. The rumor 21.____
deals with a subject which your superiors consider *confidential*.
Which of the following BEST describes how you should answer the subordinate? Tell

A. the subordinate that you don't make the rules and that he should speak to higher ranking officials
B. the subordinate that you will ask your superior for information
C. him only that you cannot comment on the matter
D. him the rumor is not true

22. Supervisors often find it difficult to *get their message across* when instructing newly appointed employees in their various duties.
The MAIN reason for this is generally that the
    A. duties of the employees have increased
    B. supervisor is often so expert in his area that he fails to see it from the learner's point of view
    C. supervisor adapts his instruction to the slowest learner in the group
    D. new employees are younger, less concerned with job security and more interested in fringe benefits

22._____

23. Assume that you are discussing a job problem with an employee under your supervision. During the discussion, you see that the man's eyes are turning away from you and that he is not paying attention.
In order to get the man's attention, you should FIRST
    A. ask him to look you in the eye
    B. talk to him about sports
    C. tell him he is being very rude
    D. change your tone of voice

23._____

24. As a supervisor, you may find it necessary to conduct meetings with your subordinates.
Of the following, which would be MOST helpful in assuring that a meeting accomplishes the purpose for which it was called?
    A. Give notice of the conclusions you would like to reach at the start of the meeting.
    B. Delay the start of the meeting until everyone is present.
    C. Write down points to be discussed in proper sequence.
    D. Make sure everyone is clear on whatever conclusions have been reached and on what must be done after the meeting.

24._____

25. Every supervisor will occasionally be called upon to deliver a reprimand to a subordinate. If done properly, this can greatly help an employee improve his performance.
Which one of the following is NOT a good practice to follow when giving a reprimand?
    A. Maintain your composure and temper
    B. Reprimand a subordinate in the presence of other employees so they can learn the same lesson
    C. Try to understand why the employee was not able to perform satisfactorily
    D. Let your knowledge of the man involved determine the exact nature of the reprimand

25._____

KEY (CORRECT ANSWERS)

1.	C	11.	A
2.	B	12.	A
3.	D	13.	B
4.	B	14.	C
5.	D	15.	A
6.	C	16.	D
7.	C	17.	A
8.	B	18.	C
9.	C	19.	B
10.	C	20.	C

21.	B
22.	B
23.	D
24.	D
25.	B

TEST 2

DIRECTIONS: Each question or incomplete statement is followed by several suggested answers or completions. Select the one that BEST answers the question or completes the statement. *PRINT THE LETTER OF THE CORRECT ANSWER IN THE SPACE AT THE RIGHT.*

1. Usually one thinks of communication as a single step, essentially that of transmitting an idea.
   Actually, however, this is only part of a total process, the FIRST step of which should be
   A. the prompt dissemination of the idea to those who may be affected by it
   B. motivating those affected to take the required action
   C. clarifying the idea in one's own mind
   D. deciding to whom the idea is to be communicated

   1.____

2. Research studies on patterns of informal communication have concluded that most individuals in a group tend to be passive recipients of news, while a few make it their business to spread it around in an organization.
   With this conclusion in mind, it would be MOST correct for the supervisor to attempt to identify these few individuals and
   A. give them the complete facts on important matters in advance of others
   B. inform the other subordinates of the identity of these few individuals so that their influence may be minimized
   C. keep them straight on the facts on important matters
   D. warn them to cease passing along any information to others

   2.____

3. The one of the following which is the PRINCIPAL advantage of making an oral report is that it
   A. affords an immediate opportunity for two-way communication between the subordinate and superior
   B. is an easy method for the superior to use in transmitting information to others of equal rank
   C. saves the time of all concerned
   D. permits more precise pinpointing of praise or blame by means of follow-up questions by the superior

   3.____

4. An agency may sometimes undertake a public relations program of a defensive nature.
   With reference to the use of defensive public relations, it would be MOST correct to state that it
   A. is bound to be ineffective since defensive statements, even though supported by factual data, can never hope to even partly overcome the effects of prior unfavorable attacks
   B. proves that the agency has failed to establish good relationships with newspapers, radio stations, or other means of publicity

   4.____

C. shows that the upper echelons of the agency have failed to develop sound public relations procedures and techniques
D. is sometimes required to aid morale by protecting the agency from unjustified criticism and misunderstanding of policies or procedures

5. Of the following factors which contribute to possible undesirable public attitudes towards an agency, the one which is MOST susceptible to being changed by the efforts of the individual employee in an organization is that
    A. enforcement of unpopular regulations as offended many individuals
    B. the organization itself has an unsatisfactory reputation
    C. the public is not interested in agency matters
    D. there are many errors in judgment committed by individual subordinates

6. It is not enough for an agency's services to be of a high quality; attention must also be given to the acceptability of these services to the general public.
This statement is GENERALLY
    A. *false*; a superior quality of service automatically wins public support
    B. *true*; the agency cannot generally progress beyond the understanding and support of the public
    C. *false*; the acceptance by the public of agency services determines their quality
    D. *true*; the agency is generally unable to engage in any effective enforcement activity without public support

7. Sustained agency participation in a program sponsored by a community organization is MOST justified when
    A. the achievement of agency objectives in some area depends partly on the activity of this organization
    B. the community organization is attempting to widen the base of participation in all community affairs
    C. the agency is uncertain as to what the community wants
    D. the agency is uncertain as to what the community wants

8. Of the following, the LEAST likely way in which a records system may serve a supervisor is in
    A. developing a sympathetic and cooperative public attitude toward the agency
    B. improving the quality of supervision by permitting a check on the accomplishment of subordinates
    C. permit a precise prediction of the exact incidences in specific categories for the following year
    D. helping to take the guesswork out of the distribution of the agency

9. Assuming that the *grapevine* in any organization is virtually indestructible, the one of the following which it is MOST important for management to understand is:
    A. What is being spread by means of the *grapevine* and the reason for spreading it
    B. What is being spread by means of the *grapevine* and how it is being spread
    C. Who is involved in spreading the information that is on the *grapevine*
    D. Why those who are involved in spreading the information are doing so

9.____

10. When the supervisor writes a report concerning an investigation to which he has been assigned, it should be LEAST intended to provide
    A. a permanent official record of relevant information gathered
    B. a summary of case findings limited to facts which tend to indicate the guilt of a suspect
    C. a statement of the facts on which higher authorities may base a corrective or disciplinary action
    D. other investigators with information so that they may continue with other phases of the investigation

10.____

11. In survey work, questionnaires rather than interviews are sometimes used. The one of the following which is a DISADVANTAGE of the questionnaire method as compared with the interview is the
    A. difficulty of accurately interpreting the results
    B. problem of maintaining anonymity of the participant
    C. fact that it is relatively uneconomical
    D. requirement of special training for the distribution of questionnaires

11.____

12. in his contacts with the public, an employee should attempt to create a good climate of support for his agency.
    This statement is GENERALLY
    A. *false*; such attempts are clearly beyond the scope of his responsibility
    B. *true*; employees of an agency who come in contact with the public have the opportunity to affect public relations
    C. *false*; such activity should be restricted to supervisors trained in public relations techniques
    D. *true*; the future expansion of the agency depends to a great extent on continued public support of the agency

12.____

13. The repeated use by a supervisor of a call for volunteers to get a job done is objectionable MAINLY because it
    A. may create a feeling of animosity between the volunteers and the non-volunteers
    B. may indicate that the supervisor is avoiding responsibility for making assignments which will be most productive
    C. is an indication that the supervisor is not familiar with the individual capabilities of his men
    D. is unfair to men who, for valid reasons, do not, or cannot volunteer

13.____

14. Of the following statements concerning subordinates' expressions to a supervisor of their opinions and feelings concerning work situations, the one which is MOST correct is that
    A. by listening and responding to such expressions the supervisor encourages the development of complaints
    B. the lack of such expressions should indicate to the supervisor that there is a high level of job satisfaction
    C. the more the supervisor listens to and responds to such expressions, the more he demonstrates lack of supervisory ability
    D. by listening and responding to such expressions, the supervisor will enable many subordinates to understand and solve their own problems on the job

14.____

15. In attempting to motivate employees, rewards are considered preferable to punishment PRIMARILY because
    A. punishment seldom has any effect on human behavior
    B. punishment usually results in decreased production
    C. supervisors find it difficult to punish
    D. rewards are more likely to result in willing cooperation

15.____

16. In an attempt to combat the low morale in his organization, a high level supervisor publicized an *open-door policy* to allow employees who wished to do so to come to him with their complaints.
    Which of the following is LEAST likely to account for the fact that no employee came in with a complaint?
    A. Employees are generally reluctant to go over the heads of their immediate supervisor.
    B. The employees did not feel that management would help them.
    C. The low morale was not due to complaints associated with the job.
    D. The employees felt that they had more to lose than to gain.

16.____

17. It is MOST desirable to use written instructions rather than oral instructions for a particular job when
    A. a mistake on the job will not be serious
    B. the job can be completed in a short time
    C. there is no need to explain the job minutely
    D. the job involves many details

17.____

18. If you receive a telephone call regarding a matter which your office does not handle, you should FIRST
    A. give the caller the telephone number of the proper office so that he can dial again
    B. offer to transfer the caller to the proper office
    C. suggest that the caller re-dial since he probably dialed incorrectly
    D. tell the caller he has reached the wrong office and then hang up

18.____

19. When you answer the telephone, the MOST important reason for identifying yourself and your organization is to
    A. give the caller time to collect his or her thoughts
    B. impress the caller with your courtesy
    C. inform the caller that he or she has reached the right number
    D. set a business-like tone at the beginning of the conversation

19.____

20. As soon as you pick up the phone, a very angry caller begins immediately to complain about city agencies and *red tape*. He says that he has been shifted to two or three different offices. It turs out that he is seeking information which is not immediately available to you. You believe, you know, however, where it can be found.
Which of the following actions is the BEST one for you to take?
    A. To eliminate all confusion, suggest that the caller write the agency stating explicitly what he wants.
    B. Apologize by telling the caller how busy city agencies now are, but also tell him directly that you do not have the information he needs.
    C. Ask for the caller's telephone number and assure him you will call back after you have checked further.
    D. Give the caller the name and telephone number of the person who might be able to help, but explain that you are not positive he will get results/

20.____

21. Which of the following approaches usually provides the BEST communication in the objectives and values of a new program which is to be introduced?
    A. A general written description of the program by the program manager for review by those who share responsibility
    B. An effective verbal presentation by the program manager to those affected
    C. Development of the plan and operational approach in carrying out the program by the program manager assisted by his key subordinates
    D. Development of the plan by the program manager's supervisor

21.____

22. What is the BEST approach for introducing change?
A
    A. combination of written and also verbal communication to all personnel affected by the change
    B. general bulletin to all personnel
    C. meeting pointing out all the values of the new approach
    D. written directive to key personnel

22.____

23. Of the following, committees are BEST used for
    A. advising the head of the organization
    B. improving functional work
    C. making executive decisions
    D. making specific planning decisions

23.____

24. An effective discussion leader is one who
    A. announces the problem and his preconceived solution at the start of the discussion
    B. guides and directs the discussion according to pre-arranged outline
    C. interrupts or corrects confused participants to save time
    D. permits anyone to say anything at any time

25. The human relations movement in management theory is basically concerned with
    A. counteracting employee unrest
    B. eliminating the *time and motion* man
    C. interrelationships among individuals in organizations
    D. the psychology of the worker

KEY (CORRECT ANSWERS)

1.	C	11.	A
2.	C	12.	B
3.	A	13.	B
4.	D	14.	D
5.	D	15.	D
6.	B	16.	C
7.	A	17.	D
8.	C	18.	B
9.	A	19.	C
10.	B	20.	C

21.	C
22.	A
23.	A
24.	B
25.	C

ARITHMETICAL REASONING
EXAMINATION SECTION
TEST 1

DIRECTIONS: Each question or incomplete statement is followed by several suggested answers or completions. Select the one that BEST answers the question or completes the statement. *PRINT THE LETTER OF THE CORRECT ANSWER IN THE SPACE AT THE RIGHT.*

1.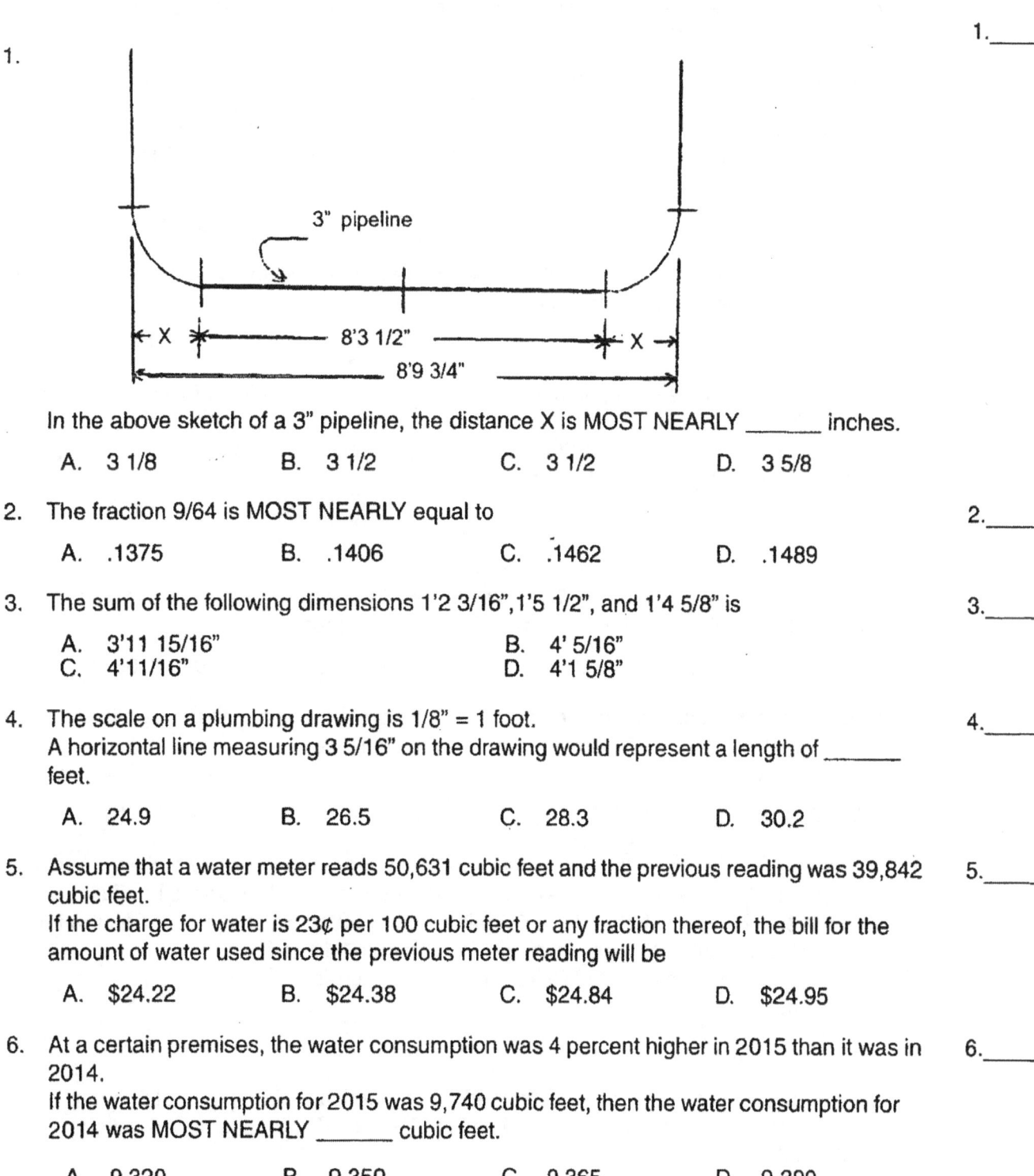

   In the above sketch of a 3" pipeline, the distance X is MOST NEARLY _____ inches.

   A. 3 1/8   B. 3 1/2   C. 3 1/2   D. 3 5/8

2. The fraction 9/64 is MOST NEARLY equal to

   A. .1375   B. .1406   C. .1462   D. .1489

3. The sum of the following dimensions 1'2 3/16", 1'5 1/2", and 1'4 5/8" is

   A. 3'11 15/16"   B. 4' 5/16"
   C. 4'11/16"   D. 4'1 5/8"

4. The scale on a plumbing drawing is 1/8" = 1 foot.
   A horizontal line measuring 3 5/16" on the drawing would represent a length of _____ feet.

   A. 24.9   B. 26.5   C. 28.3   D. 30.2

5. Assume that a water meter reads 50,631 cubic feet and the previous reading was 39,842 cubic feet.
   If the charge for water is 23¢ per 100 cubic feet or any fraction thereof, the bill for the amount of water used since the previous meter reading will be

   A. $24.22   B. $24.38   C. $24.84   D. $24.95

6. At a certain premises, the water consumption was 4 percent higher in 2015 than it was in 2014.
   If the water consumption for 2015 was 9,740 cubic feet, then the water consumption for 2014 was MOST NEARLY _____ cubic feet.

   A. 9,320   B. 9,350   C. 9,365   D. 9,390

7. A pump delivers water at a constant rate of 40 gallons per minute.
   If there are 7.5 gallons to a cubic foot of water, the time it will take to fill a tank 6 feet x 5 feet x 4 feet is MOST NEARLY _____ minutes.

   A. 15 B. 22.5 C. 28.5 D. 30

8. The total weight, in pounds, of three lengths of 3" cast-iron pipe 7'6" long, weighing 14.5 pounds per foot, and four lengths of 4" cast-iron pipe each 5'0" long, weighing 13.0 pounds per foot, is MOST NEARLY

   A. 540 B. 585 C. 600 D. 665

9. The water pressure at the bottom of a column of water 34 feet high is 14.7 lbs./sq.in. The water pressure in lbs./sq.in. at the bottom of the column of water 12 feet high is MOST NEARLY

   A. 3 B. 5 C. 7 D. 9

10. The number of cubic yards of earth that would be removed when digging a trench 8 feet wide x 9 feet deep x 63 feet long is

    A. 56 B. 168 C. 314 D. 504

11. On test, a meter registered one cubic foot for each 1 1/3 cubic feet of water that passed through it.
    If the meter had a reading of 1,200 cubic feet, we may conclude that the CORRECT amount should be _____ cubic feet.

    A. 800 B. 900 C. 1,500 D. 1,600

12. A water use meter reads 87,463 cubic feet.
    If the previous reading was 17,377 cubic feet and the rate charged is 15 cents per 100 cubic feet, the bill for water use during this period is about

    A. $45.00 B. $65.00 C. $85.00 D. $105.00

13. Under proper conditions, the one of the following groups of pipes that gives the same flow in gals/min as one 6" diameter pipe is (neglect friction) _____ pipes of _____ diameter each.

    A. 3; 3" B. 4; 3" C. 2; 4" D. 3; 4"

14. A roof tank is used to furnish the domestic water supply to a ten story building. This tank has a capacity of 5,900 gallons. At 10:00 A.M. one morning, the tank is half full.
    If water is being used at the rate of 50 gals/min, the pump which is used to fill the tank has a rated capacity of 90 gals/min, the time it would take to fill the tank under these conditions is MOST NEARLY _____ hour(s), _____ minutes.

    A. 2; 8 B. 1; 14 C. 2; 32 D. 1; 2

15. The number of gallons of water contained in a cylindrical swimming pool 8 feet in diameter and filled to a depth of 3 feet 6 inches is MOST NEARLY (assume 7.5 gallons = 1 cubic foot)

    A. 30 B. 225 C. 1,320 D. 3,000

16. The charge for metered water is 52 1/2 cents per hundred cubic feet, with a minimum charge of $21 per annum. Of the following, the SMALLEST water usage in hundred cubic feet that would result in a charge GREATER than the minimum is

    A. 39   B. 40   C. 41   D. 42

17. The annual frontage rent on a one-story building 40 ft. in length is $735.00. For each additional story, $52.50 per annum is added to the frontage rent. For demolition, the charge for wetting down is 3/8 of the annual frontage charge.
    The charge for wetting down a building six stories in height, with a 40 ft. frontage, is MOST NEARLY

    A. $369   B. $371   C. $372   D. $374

18. If the drawing of a piping layout is made to a scale of 1/4" equals one foot, then a 7'9" length of piping would be represented by a scaled length on the drawing of APPROXIMATELY _____ inches.

    A. 2   B. 7 3/4   C. 23 1/4   D. 31

19. A plumbing sketch is drawn to a scale of eighth-size. A line measuring 3" on the sketch would be equivalent to _____ feet.

    A. 2   B. 6   C. 12   D. 24

20. If 500 feet of pipe weighs 800 lbs., the number of pounds that 120 feet will weigh is MOST NEARLY

    A. 190   B. 210   C. 230   D. 240

21. If a trench is excavated 3'0" wide by 5'6" deep and 50 feet long, the total number of cubic yards of earth removed is MOST NEARLY

    A. 30   B. 90   C. 150   D. 825

22. Assume that a plumber earns $86,500 per year.
    If eighteen percent of his pay is deducted for taxes and social security, his net weekly pay will be APPROXIMATELY

    A. $1,326   B. $1,365   C. $1,436   D. $1,457.50

23. Assume that a plumbing installation is made up of the following fixtures and groups of fixtures: 12 bathroom groups each containing one W.C., one lavatory, and one bathtub with shower; 12 bathroom groups each containing one W.C., one lavatory, one bathtub, and one shower stall; 24 combination kitchen fixtures; 4 floor drains; 6 slop sinks without flushing rim; and 2 shower stalls (or shower bath).
    The total number of fixtures for the above plumbing installation is MOST NEARLY

    A. 60   B. 95   C. 120   D. 210

24. A triangular opening in a wall forms a 30-60 degree right triangle.
    If the longest side measures 12'0", then the shortest side will measure

    A. 3'0"   B. 4'0"   C. 6'0"   D. 8'0"

25. You are directed to cut 4 pieces of pipe, one each of the following length: 2'6 1/4", 3'9 3/8", 4'7 5/8", and 5'8 7/8".
The total length of these 4 pieces is

    A. 15'7 1/4"   B. 15'9 3/8"   C. 16'5 7/8"   D. 16'8 1/8"

KEY (CORRECT ANSWERS)

1.	A	11.	D
2.	B	12.	D
3.	B	13.	B
4.	B	14.	B
5.	C	15.	C
6.	C	16.	C
7.	B	17.	D
8.	B	18.	A
9.	B	19.	A
10.	B	20.	A

21. A
22. B
23. C
24. C
25. D

SOLUTIONS TO PROBLEMS

1. 8'3 1/2" + x + x = 8'9 3/4" Then, 2x = 6 1/4", so x = 3 1/8"

2. 9/64 = .140625 = .1406

3. 1'2 3/16" + 1'5 1/2" +1'4 5/8" = 3'11 21/16" = 4'5/16"

4. 3 5/16" ÷ 1/8" =53/16 x 8/1 = 26.5. Then, (26.5)(1 ft.) = 26.5 feet

5. 50,631 - 39,842 = 10,789; 10,789 ÷ 100 = 107.89
   Since the cost is .23 per 100 cubic feet or any fraction thereof, the cost will be
   (.23)(107) + .23 = $24.84

6. 9740 ÷ 1.04 = 9365 cu.ft.

7. 40 ÷ 7.5 = 5 1/3 cu.ft. of water per minute. The volume = (6)(5)(4) = 120 cu.ft. Thus, the number of minutes needed to fill the tank is 120 ÷ 5 1/3 = 22.5

8. 3" pipe: 3 x 7'6" = 22 1/2' x 14.5 lbs. = 326.25
   4" pipe: 4 x 5' = 20' x 13 lbs. = 260
   326.25 + 260 = 586.25 (most nearly 585)

9. Let x = pressure. Then, 34/12 = 14.7/x. So, 34x = 176.4
   Solving, x ≈ 5 lbs./sq.in.

10. (8)(9)(63) = 4536 cu.ft. Since 1 cu.yd. = 27 cu.ft., 4536 cu.ft. is equivalent to 168 cu.yds.

11. Let x = correct amount. Then, $\dfrac{1}{1200} = \dfrac{1\frac{1}{3}}{x}$. Solving, x = 1600

12. 87,463 - 17,377 = 70,086; and 70,086 ÷ 100 = 700.86 ≈ 700 Then, (700)(.15) = $105.00

13. Cross-sectional area of a 6" diameter pipe = $(\pi)(3")^2 = 9\pi$ sq. in. Note that the combined cross-sectional areas of four 3" diameter pipes = $(4)(\pi)(1.5")^2 = 9\pi$ sq. in.

14. 90 - 50 = 40 gals/min. Then, 2950 ÷ 40 = 73.75 min. ≈ 1 hr. 14 min.

15. Volume = $(\pi)(4)^2(3\ 1/2) = 56\pi$ cu.ft. Then, $(56\pi)(7.5)$ = 1320 gals.

16. For 4100 cu.ft., the charge of (.525)(41) = $21,525 > $21

17. Rent = $73,500 + (5)($52.50) = $997,50. For demolition, the charge = (3/8)($997.50)
    $374

18. (1/4")(7.75) = 2"

19. (3")(8) = 24" = 2 ft.

20. Let x = weight. Then, 500/800 = 120/x . Solving, x = 192 190 lbs.

21. (3')(5 1/2')(50') = 825 cu.ft. Then, 825 ÷ 27 ≈ 30 cu.yds.

22. Net pay = (.82)($86,500) = $70,930/yr. Weekly pay = $70,930 ÷ 52 ≈ $1365

23. (12x3) + (12x4) +24+4+6+2= 120

24. The shortest side = (1/2)(hypotenuse) = (1/2)(12') = 6'

25. 2'6 1/4" + 3'9 3/8" + 4'7 5/8" + 5'8 7/8 " = 14'30 17/8" = 16'8 1/8"

TEST 2

DIRECTIONS: Each question or incomplete statement is followed by several suggested answers or completions. Select the one that BEST answers the question or completes the statement. *PRINT THE LETTER OF THE CORRECT ANSWER IN THE SPACE AT THE RIGHT.*

1. The sum of the following pipe lengths, 15 5/8", 8 3/4", 30 5/16" and 20 1/2", is 1.____
   A. 77 1/8"   B. 76 3/16"   C. 75 3/16"   D. 74 5/16"

2. If the outside diameter of a pipe is 6 inches and the wall thickness is 1/2 inch, the inside area of this pipe, in square inches, is MOST NEARLY 2.____
   A. 15.7   B. 17.3   C. 19.6   D. 23.8

3. Three lengths of pipe 1'10", 3'2 1/2", and 5'7 1/2", respectively, are to be cut from a pipe 14'0" long. 3.____
   Allowing 1/8" for each pipe cut, the length of pipe remaining is
   A. 3'1 1/8"   B. 3'2 1/2"   C. 3'3 1/4"   D. 3'3 5/8"

4. According to the building code, the MAXIMUM permitted surface temperature of combustible construction materials located near heating equipment is 76.5°C. (°F=(°Cx9/5)+32) Maximum temperature Fahrenheit is MOST NEARLY 4.____
   A. 170° F   B. 195° F   C. 210° F   D. 220° F

5. A pump discharges 7.5 gals/minutes. 5.____
   In 2.5 hours the pump will discharge _____ gallons.
   A. 1125   B. 1875   C. 1950   D. 2200

6. A pipe with an outside diameter of 4" has a circumference of MOST NEARLY _____ inches. 6.____
   A. 8.05   B. 9.81   C. 12.57   D. 14.92

7. A piping sketch is drawn to a scale of 1/8" = 1 foot. 7.____
   A vertical steam line measuring 3 1/2" on the sketch would have an ACTUAL length of _____ feet.
   A. 16   B. 22   C. 24   D. 28

8. A pipe having an inside diameter of 3.48 inches and a wall thickness of .18 inches will have an outside diameter of _____ inches. 8.____
   A. 3.84   B. 3.64   C. 3.57   D. 3.51

9. A rectangular steel bar having a volume of 30 cubic inches, a width of 2 inches, and a height of 3 inches will have a length of _____ inches. 9.____
   A. 12   B. 10   C. 8   D. 5

10. A pipe weighs 20.4 pounds per foot of length. 10.____
    The total weight of eight pieces of this pipe with each piece 20 feet in length is MOST NEARLY _____ pounds.
    A. 460   B. 1,680   C. 2,420   D. 3,260

11. Assume that four pieces of pipe measuring 2'1 1/4", 4'2 3/4", 5'1 9/16", and 6'3 5/8", respectively, are cut with a saw from a pipe 20'0" long.
Allowing 1/16" waste for each cut, the length of the remaining pipe is

   A. 2'1 9/16"   B. 2'2 9/16"   C. 2'4 13/16"   D. 2'8 9/16"

12. If one cubic inch of steel weighs 0.28 pounds, the weight, in pounds, of a steel bar 1/2" x 6" x 2'0" long is MOST NEARLY

   A. 11   B. 16   C. 20   D. 24

13. If the circumference of a circle is equal to 31.416 inches, then its diameter, in inches, is equal to MOST NEARLY

   A. 8   B. 9   C. 10   D. 13

14. Assume that a steam fitter's helper receives a salary of $171.36 a day for 250 days is considered a full work year. If taxes, social security, hospitalization, and pension deducted from his salary amounts to 16 percent of his gross pay, then his net yearly salary will be MOST NEARLY

   A. $31,788   B. $35,982   C. $41,982   D. $42,840

15. If the outside diameter of a pipe is 14 inches and the wall thickness is 1/2 inch, then the inside area of the pipe, in square inches, is MOST NEARLY

   A. 125   B. 133   C. 143   D. 154

16. A steam leak in a pipe line allows steam to escape at a rate of 50,000 pounds each month.
Assuming that the cost of steam is $2.50 per 1,000 pounds, the TOTAL cost of wasted steam from this leak for a 12-month period would amount to

   A. $125   B. $300   C. $1,500   D. $3,000

17. If 250 feet of 4" pipe weighs 400 pounds, the weight of this pipe per linear foot is _____ pounds.

   A. 1.25   B. 1.50   C. 1.60   D. 1.75

18. A set of heating plan drawings is drawn to a scale of 1/4" = 1 foot.
If a length of pipe measures 4 5/8" on the drawing, the ACTUAL length of the pipe, in feet, is

   A. 16.3   B. 16.8   C. 17.5   D. 18.5

19. The TOTAL length of four pieces of pipe whose lengths are 3'4 1/2", 2'1 5/16", 4'9 3/8", and 2'3 1/4", respectively, is

   A. 11'5 7/16"   B. 11'6 7/16"
   C. 12'5 7/16"   D. 12'6 7/16"

20. Assume that a pipe trench is 3 feet wide, 3 feet deep, and 300 feet long.
If the unit cost of excavating the trench is $120 per cubic yard, the TOTAL cost of excavating the trench is

   A. $1,200   B. $12,000   C. $27,000   D. $36,000

21. The TOTAL length of four pieces of 1 1/2" galvanized steel pipe whose lengths are 7 ft. + 3 1/2 inches, 4 ft. + 2 1/4 inches, 6 ft. + 7 inches, and 8 ft. +5 1/8 inches is 21._____

    A. 26 feet + 5 7/8 inches
    B. 25 ft. + 6 7/8 inches
    C. 25 feet + 4 1/4 inches
    D. 25 ft. + 3 3/8 inches

22. A swimming pool is 25' wide by 75' long and has an average depth of 5'. 1 cubic foot contains 7.5 gallons of water. The capacity, when filled to the overflow, is _____ gallons. 22._____

    A. 9,375   B. 65,625   C. 69,005   D. 70,312

23. The sum of 3 1/4, 5 1/8, 2 1/2, and 3 3/8 is 23._____

    A. 14   B. 14 1/8   C. 14 1/4   D. 14 3/8

24. Assume that it takes 6 men 8 days to do a particular job. If you have only 4 men available to do this job and they all work at the same speed, then the number of days it would take to complete the job would be 24._____

    A. 11   B. 12   C. 13   D. 14

25. The total length of four pieces of 2" O.D. pipe, whose lengths are 7'3 1/2", 4'2 3/16", 5'7 5/16", and 8'5 7/8", respectively, is MOST NEARLY 25._____

    A. 24'6 3/4"
    B. 24'7 15/16"
    C. 25'5 13/16"
    D. 25'6 7/8"

KEY (CORRECT ANSWERS)

1. C		11. B	
2. C		12. C	
3. D		13. C	
4. A		14. B	
5. A		15. B	
6. C		16. C	
7. D		17. C	
8. A		18. D	
9. D		19. D	
10. D		20. B	

    21. A
    22. D
    23. C
    24. B
    25. D

SOLUTIONS TO PROBLEMS

1. 15 5/8" + 8 3/4" + 30 5/16" + 20 1/2" = 73 35/16" = 75 3/16"

2. Inside diameter = 6" - 1/2" - 1/2" = 5". Area = $(\pi)(5/2")^2 \approx$ 19.6 sq. in.

3. Pipe remaining = 14' - 1'10" - 3'2 1/2" - 5'7 1/2" - (3)(1/8") = 3'3 5/8"

4. 76.5 x 9/5 = 137.7 + 32 = 169.7

5. 7.5 x 150 = 1125

6. Radius = 2" Circumference = $(2\pi)(2")\approx$ 12.57"

7. 3 1/2" 1/8" = (7/2)(8/1) = 28 Then, (28)(1 ft.) = 28 feet

8. Outside diameter = 3.48" + .18" + .18" = 3.84"

9. 30 = (2)(3)(length). So, length = 5"

10. Total weight = (20.4)(8)(20) $\approx$ 3260 lbs.

11. 20' - 2'1 1/4" - 4'2 3/4" - 5'1 9/16" - 6'3 5/8" - (4)(1/16") = 2'2 9/16"

12. Weight = (.28)(1/2")(6")(24") = 20.16 $\approx$ 20 lbs.

13. Diameter = 31.416" ÷ $\pi \approx$ 10"

14. His net pay for 250 days = (.84)($171.36)(250) = $35,985.60 $\approx$ $35,928 (from answer key)

15. Inside diameter = 14" - 1/2" - 1/2" = 13". Area = $(\pi)(13/2")^2 \approx$ 133 sq.in

16. (50,000 lbs.)(12) = 600,000 lbs. per year. The cost would be ($2.50)(600) = $1500

17. 400 ÷ 250 = 1.60 pounds per linear foot

18. 4 5/8" ÷ 1/4" = 37/8 . 4/1 = 18.5 Then, (18.5)(1 ft.) = 18.5 feet

19. 3'4 1/2" + 2'1 5/16" + 4'9 3/8" + 2'3 1/4" = 11'17 23/16" = 12'6 7/16"

20. (3')(3')(300') = 2700 cu.ft., which is 2700 ÷ 27 = 100 cu.yds. Total cost = ($120)(100) = $12,000

21. 7'3 1/2" + 4'2 1/4" + 6'7" + 8'5 1/8" = 25'17 7/8" = 26'5 7/8"

22. (25)(75)(5) = 9375 cu.ft. Then, (9375)(7.5) $\approx$ 70,312 gals.

23. 3 1/4 + 5 1/8 + 2 1/2 + 3 3/8 = 13 10/8 = 14 1/4

24. (6) (8) = 48 man-days. Then, 48 ÷ 4 = 12 days

25. 7'3 1/2" + 4'2 3/16" + 5'7 5/16" + 8'5 7/8"= 24'17 30/16" = 25'6 7/8"

TEST 3

DIRECTIONS: Each question or incomplete statement is followed by several suggested answers or completions. Select the one that BEST answers the question or completes the statement. *PRINT THE LETTER OF THE CORRECT ANSWER IN THE SPACE AT THE RIGHT.*

1. The time required to pump 2,500 gallons of water out of a sump at the rate of 12 1/2 gallons per minutes would be _____ hour(s) _____ minutes. 1._____

    A. 1; 40   B. 2; 30   C. 3; 20   D. 6; 40

2. Copper tubing which has an inside diameter of 1 1/16" and a wall thickness of .095" has an outside diameter which is MOST NEARLY _____ inches. 2._____

    A. 1 5/32   B. 1 3/16   C. 1 7/32   D. 1 1/4

3. Assume that 90 gallons per minute flow through a certain 3-inch pipe which is tapped into a street main. 3._____
   The amount of water which would flow through a 1-inch pipe tapped into the same street main is MOST NEARLY _____ gpm.

    A. 90   B. 45   C. 30   D. 10

4. The weight of a 6 foot length of 8-inch pipe which weighs 24.70 pounds per foot is _____ lbs. 4._____

    A. 148.2   B. 176.8   C. 197.6   D. 212.4

5. If a 4-inch pipe is directly coupled to a 2-inch pipe and 16 gallons per minute are flowing through the 4-inch pipe, then the flow through the 2-inch pipe will be _____ gallons per minute. 5._____

    A. 4   B. 8   C. 16   D. 32

6. If the water pressure at the bottom of a column of water 34 feet high is 14.7 pounds per square inch, the water pressure at the bottom of a column of water 18 feet high is MOST NEARLY _____ pounds per square inch. 6._____

    A. 8.0   B. 7.8   C. 7.6   D. 7.4

7. If there are 7 1/2 gallons in a cubic foot of water and if water flows from a hose at a constant rate of 4 gallons per minute, the time it should take to COMPLETELY fill a tank of 1,600 cubic feet capacity with water from that hose is _____ hours. 7._____

    A. 300   B. 150   C. 100   D. 50

8. Each of a group of fifteen water meter readers read an average of 62 water meters a day in a certain 5-day work week. A total of 5,115 meters are read by this group the following week. 8._____
   The TOTAL number of meters read in the second week as compared to the first week shows a

    A. 10% increase   B. 15% increase
    C. 20% increase   D. 5% decrease

9. A certain water consumer used 5% more water in 1994 than he did in 1993. If his water consumption for 1994 was 8,375 cubic feet, the amount of water he consumed in 1993 was MOST NEARLY _____ cubic feet.

   A. 9,014   B. 8,816   C. 7,976   D. 6,776

10. Assume that a water meter reads 40,175 cubic feet and that the previous reading was 29,186 cubic feet.
    If the charge for water is 92 cents per 100 cubic feet or any fraction thereof, the bill for the amount of water used since the previous meter reading should be

    A. $100.28   B. $101.04   C. $101.08   D. $101.20

11. A leaking faucet caused a loss of 216 cubic feet of water in a 30-day month. If there are 7.5 gallons in a cubic foot of water, then the AVERAGE loss of water per hour for that month was _____ gallons.

    A. 2 1/4   B. 2 1/8   C. 2   D. 1 3/4

12. The fraction which is equal to .375 is

    A. 3/16   B. 5/32   C. 3/8   D. 5/12

13. A square backyard swimming pool, each side of which is 10 feet long, is filled to a depth of 3 1/2 feet.
    If there are 7 1/2 gallons in a cubic foot of water, the number of gallons of water in the pool is MOST NEARLY _____ gallons.

    A. 46.7   B. 100   C. 2,625   D. 3,500

14. When 1 5/8, 3 3/4, 6 1/3, and 9 1/2 are added, the resulting sum is

    A. 21 1/8   B. 21 1/6   C. 21 5/24   D. 21 1/4

15. When 946 1/2 is subtracted from 1,035 1/4, the result is

    A. 87 1/4   B. 87 3/4   C. 88 1/4   D. 88 3/4

16. When 39 is multiplied by 697, the result is

    A. 8,364   B. 26,283   C. 27,183   D. 28,003

17. When 16.074 is divided by .045, the result is

    A. 3.6   B. 35.7   C. 357.2   D. 3,572

18. To dig a trench 3'0" wide, 50'0" long, and 5'6" deep, the total number of cubic yards of earth to be removed is MOST NEARLY

    A. 30   B. 90   C. 140   D. 825

19. The TOTAL length of four pieces of 2" pipe, whose lengths are 7'3 1/2", 4'2 3/16", 5'7 5/16", and 8'5 7/8", respectively, is

    A. 24'6 3/4"   B. 24'7 15/16"
    C. 25'5 13/16"   D. 25'6 7/8"

20. A hot water line made of copper has a straight horizontal run of 150 feet and, when installed, is at a temperature of 45° F. In use, its temperature rises to 190° F.
    If the coefficient of expansion for copper is 0.0000095" per foot per degree F, the TOTAL expansion, in inches, in the run of pipe is given by the product of 150 multiplied by 0.0000095 by

    A. 145
    B. 145 x 12
    C. 145 divided by 12
    D. 145 x 12 x 12

21. A water storage tank measures 5' long, 4' wide, and 6' deep and is filled to the 5 1/2' mark with water.
    If one cubic foot of water weighs 62 pounds, the number of pounds of water required to COMPLETELY fill the tank is

    A. 7,440
    B. 6,200
    C. 1,240
    D. 620

22. Assume that a pipe worker earns $83,125.00 per year.
    If seventeen percent of his pay is deducted for taxes, social security, and pension, his net weekly pay will be APPROXIMATELY

    A. $1598.50
    B. $1504.00
    C. $1453.00
    D. $1325.00

23. If eighteen feet of 4" cast iron pipe weighs approximately 390 pounds, the weight of this pipe per lineal foot will be MOST NEARLY _____ lbs.

    A. 19
    B. 22
    C. 23
    D. 25

24. If it takes 3 men 11 days to dig a trench, the number of days it will take 5 men to dig the same trench, assuming all work is done at the same rate of speed, is MOST NEARLY

    A. 6 1/2
    B. 7 3/4
    C. 8 1/4
    D. 8 3/4

25. If a trench is dug 6'0" deep, 2'6" wide, and 8'0" long, the area of the opening, in square feet, is MOST NEARLY

    A. 48
    B. 32
    C. 20
    D. 15

KEY (CORRECT ANSWERS)

1.	C	11.	A
2.	D	12.	C
3.	D	13.	C
4.	A	14.	C
5.	B	15.	D
6.	B	16.	C
7.	D	17.	C
8.	A	18.	A
9.	C	19.	D
10.	D	20.	A

21. D
22. D
23. B
24. A
25. C

SOLUTIONS TO PROBLEMS

1. 2500 ÷ 12 1/2 = 200 min. = 3 hrs. 20 min.

2. 1 1/16" + .095" + .095" = 1.0625 + .095 + .095 = 1.2525" ≈ 1 1/4"

3. Cross-sectional areas for a 3-inch pipe and a 1-inch pipe are $(\pi)(1.5)^2$ and $(\pi)(.5)^2$ = 2.25π and $.25\pi$, respectively. Let x = amount of water flowing through the 1-inch pipe. Then, $\frac{90}{x} = \frac{2.25\pi}{.25\pi}$. Solving, x = 10 gals/min

4. (24.70)(6) = 148.2 lbs.

5. $\frac{4" \text{ pipe}}{16 \text{ gallons}} = \frac{2" \text{ pipe}}{x \text{ gallons}}$, 4x = 32, x = 8

6. Let x = pressure. Then, 34/18 = 14.7/x. Solving, x ≈ 7.8

7. (1600)(7.5) = 12,000 gallons. Then, 12,000 ÷ 4 = 3000 min. = 50 hours

8. (15)(62)(5) = 4650. Then, (5115-4650)/4650 = 10% increase

9. 8375 ÷ 1.05 ≈ 7976 cu.ft.

10. 40,175 - 29,186 = 10,989 cu.ft. Then, 10,989 100 = 109.89. Since .92 is charged for each 100 cu.ft. or fraction thereof, total cost = (.92)(110) = $101.20

11. (216)(7.5) = 1620 gallons. In 30 days, there are 720 hours. Thus, the average water loss per hour = 1620 ÷ 720 = 2 1/4 gallons.

12. .375 = 375/1000 = 3/8

13. Volume = (10)(10)(3 1/2) = 350 cu.ft. Then, (350)(7 1/2) = 2625 gallons

14. 1 5/8 + 3 3/4 + 6 1/3 + 9 1/2 = 19 53/24 = 21 5/24

15. 1035 1/4 - 946 1/2 = 88 3/4

16. (39)(697) = 27,183

17. 16.074 .045 = 357.2

18. (3')(50')(5 1/2') = 825 cu.ft. ≈ 30 cu.yds., since 1 cu.yd. = 27 cu.ft.

19. 7'3 1/2" + 4'2 3/16" + 5'7 5/16" + 8'5 7/8" = 24'17 30/16" = 25'6 7/8"

20. Total expansion = (150)(.0000095)(145)

21. Number of pounds needed = (5)(4)(6-5 1/2)(62) = 620

22. Net annual pay = ($83,125)(.83) ≈ $69000. Then, the net weekly pay = $69000 ÷ 52 ≈ $1325 (actually about $1327)

23. 390 lbs. ÷ 18 = 21.6 lbs. per linear foot

24. (3)(11) = 33 man-days. Then, 33 ÷ 5 = 6.6 ≈ 6 1/2 days

25. Area = (8')(2 1/2') = 20 sq.ft.

ARITHMETIC OF SEWAGE TREATMENT

The English system of measurements is used for computations at sewage treatment works, except in the case of a few determinations. The metric system will be mentioned where the metric units are used.

Basic Units

Linear	1 inch (in.)	= 2.540 centimeters (cm)
	1 foot (ft.)	= 12 inches (in.)
	1 yard (yd.)	= 3 feet (ft.)
	1 mile	= 5,280 feet
	1 meter (m)	= 39.37 in. = 3.281 ft.
		= 1.094 yd.
	1 meter	= 100 centimeters
Area	1 square foot (sq. ft.)	= 144 square inches (sq. in.)
	1 square yard (sq. yd.)	= 9 sq. ft.
	1 acre	= 43,560 sq. ft.
	1 square mile	= 640 acres
Volume	1 cubic foot	= 1728 cubic inches (cu. in.)
	1 cubic yard	= 27 cu. ft.
	1 cubic foot	= 7.48 gallons
	1 gallon (gal.)	= 231 cu. in.
	1 gallon	= 4 quarts (qt)
	1 gallon	= 3.785 liters(1)
	1 liter	= 1000 milliliters (ml)
Weight	1 pound (lb.)	= 16 ounces = 7000 grains
		= 453.6 grams
	1 ounce	= 28.35 grams (g)
	1 kilogram	= 1000 grams
	1 gram	=1000 milligrams (mg)
	1 cu. ft. water	= 62.4 pounds
	1 gallon water	= 8.33 pounds
	1 liter water	= 1 kilogram
	1 milliliter water	= 1 gram

Definition of Terms

A *ratio* is the indicated division of two pure numbers. As such is indicates the relative magnitude of two quantities. The ratio of 2 to 3 is written 2/3.

A *pure* number is used without reference to any particular thing.

A *concrete* number applies to a particular thing and is the product of a pure number and a physical unit. 5 ft. means 5 times 1 ft. or 5 X (1 ft.).

Rate units are formed when one physical unit is divided by another.

$$\frac{60 \text{ft.}}{2 \text{sec.}} = 30 \frac{\text{(ft.)}}{\text{(sec.)}}$$

Physical units can be formed by multiplying two or more other physical units.

1 ft. X 1 ft. = 1 ft. X ft. = 1 ft.^{2} (square foot)

Physical units may cancel each other.

$$\frac{6 \text{ ft} \times 7.48 \text{ gallons}}{1 \text{ ft.}} = 6 \times 7.48 \text{ gallons}$$

Per cent means per 100 and is the numerator of a fraction whose denominator is always 100. It may be expressed by the symbol "%". The word *per* refers to a fraction whose numerator precedes *per* and whose denominator follows. Hence "per" means "divided by." It is often indicated by a sloping line as "/."

Problem: What is 15 per cent of 60?

$$60 \times \frac{15}{100} = \frac{900}{100} = 9$$

Problem: One pound of lime is stirred into one gallon of water.

What is the per cent of lime in the slurry?

$$\frac{1}{1+8.33} \times 100 = \frac{100}{1+8.33} = 10.7 \text{ per cent}$$

Formulas

Circumference of a circle = $\Pi D = 2\Pi R$

Area of a circle $= \Pi R^2 = \dfrac{\Pi D^2}{4}$

$\Pi = 3.1416$
Area of triangle = 1/2 base X altitude
Area of rectangle = base X altitude
Cylindrical area = circumference of base X length
Volume of cylinder = area of base X length
Volume of rectangular tank = area of bottom X depth
Volume of cone = 1/3 X area of base X height
Velocity = distance divided by time. Inches, feet, or miles divided by hours, minutes, or seconds.
  Discharge = volume of flow divided by time.
    Gallons or cubic feet divided by days, hours, minutes, or seconds.
    1 cu. ft. per sec. = 647,000 gallons per day.
    1 mgd = 1.54 cfs = 92.4 cfm

Detention Time. The theoretical time equals the volume of tank divided by the flow per unit time. The flow volume and tank volume must be in the same units.

$$\frac{20,000 \text{ gal}}{200 \; \dfrac{\text{gal}}{\text{min.}}} = 100 \text{ minutes}$$

Problem: A tank is 60 X 20 X 30 ft. The flow is 5 mgd.

What is the detention time in hours?

1 mgd = 92.4 cfm

$$\frac{60 \text{ ft.} \times 20 \text{ ft.} \times 30 \text{ ft.}}{92.4 \times 5 \frac{\text{ft}^3}{\text{min}}} = 78 \text{ min. or 1 hr. and 18 min. or 1.3 hours}$$

Surface Settling Rate:

This means gallons per square foot of tank surface per day.

Problem: If the daily flow is 0.5 mgd and the tank is 50 ft. long and 12 ft. wide, calculate the surface settling rate.

$$\frac{500,000 \text{ gal./day}}{50 \text{ ft.} \times 12 \text{ ft.}} = \frac{833 \text{ gal.}}{\text{ft.}^2 \times \text{day}}$$

Weir Overflow Rate:

This means gallons per day per foot length of weir.

Problem: A circular settling tank is 90 ft. in diameter. The flow is 3.0 mgd. Calculate the weir overflow rate.

$$\frac{3,000,000 \text{ gal./day}}{\Pi \times 90 \text{ ft.}} = \frac{10,600 \text{ gal}}{\text{ft.} \times \text{day}}$$

Rate of Filtration: The mgd is divided by the acres of stone to give

$$\frac{mg}{\text{acre} \times \text{day}} = \text{mgad}$$

$$\frac{mg}{\text{acre} \times \text{ft.} \times \text{day}} = \text{mgaftd}$$

An acre-ft. is an acre in area and 1 ft. deep.
A fixed-nozzle filter is 140 x 125 feet. Stone is six feet deep. Flow is 9 mgd. Calculate the rate of dosing or hydraulic loading in mg per acre-foot per day.

$$\frac{140 \times 125}{43560} = \text{acres} = 0.402$$

$$0.402 \times 6 = 2.412 \text{ acre-feet}$$

$$\frac{9}{2.412} = \frac{mg}{\text{acre} \times \text{ft.} \times \text{day}} = 3.73$$

The BOD of a settling tank effluent is 200 ppm. If 15 lb. of BOD per 1000 ft.^{3} of stone is to be the organic loading, how many cubic feet of stone are necessary with a hydraulic loading of 3 mgd.

$$\frac{200 \times 8.33 \times 3 \times 1000}{15} = 333,333 \text{ ft.}^3$$

$$\frac{333,333}{6} = 55,500 \text{ ft.}^2 \text{ for filter area if stone is 6 ft. deep.}$$

Parts per million:

This is a weight ratio. Any unit may be used; pounds per million pounds or milligrams per liter if the liquid has a specific gravity equal to water or very nearly so. 1 liter of water = 1,000,000 milligrams.

   1 ppm = 8.33 lbs. per million gallons
   1 ppm = 1 milligram per liter

A sewage with 600 ppm suspended solids has 600 X 8.33 = 4998 lb. of suspended solids per million gallons.

Efficiency of Removal:

$$\frac{\text{ppm influent} - \text{ppm efflueny}}{\text{ppm influent}} \cdot 100 = \text{percent efficiency of removal}$$

Percent of Moisture:

$$\frac{\text{wt. of wet sludge} - \text{wt. of day sludge}}{\text{wt. of wet sludge}} \cdot 100 = \text{percent moisture}$$

Percent of Dry solids:

$$\frac{\text{wt. of day sludge}}{\text{wt. of wet sludge}} \cdot 100 = \text{parcent day solids}$$

Other calculated quantities that need no special explanation are:
   Square feet of sludge drying bed per capita
   Cubic feet of digestion space per capita
   Cubic feet of sludge produced per day per capita
   Cubic feet of grit per million gallons
   Pounds of sludge per capita per day
   Cubic feet of gas per capita per day
   Kilowatt-hours per million gallons pumped

Specific Gravity: This is the ratio of the density of a substance to the density of water. There is no unit. Density = the weight of unit volume.

$$\text{S.G.} = \frac{(\text{wt. bottle with sludge}) - (\text{wt. of empty bottle})}{(\text{wt. bottle with water}) - (\text{wt. of empty bottle})}$$

1 gallon of water = 8.33 lbs.
1 cu. ft. of water = 62.4 lbs.
These vary slightly with temperature.
   Water at 32° F. = 62.417 lb./ft.^{3}

Water at 62° F. = 62.355 lb./ft.³
Water at 212° F. = 59.7 lb./ft.³
Ice   = 57.5 lb./ft.³

Problem: What is the weight of dry solids in 1000 gallons of 10% sludge whose specific gravity is 1.04?

$$1000 \times 8.33 \times 1.40 \times \frac{10}{100} = 866.3 \text{ lbs.}$$

Mixtures:

If two materials of different percentages are to be mixed to produce an intermediate percentage, it may be done by rectangle method. Problem: We have 30 per cent and 50 per cent material. In what ratio shall they be mixed to produce 37 per cent material.

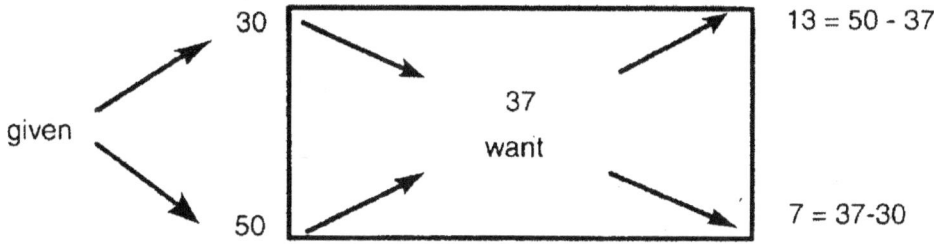

Desired ration is 13 parts of the 30 per cent and 7 parts of the 50 per cent. This will give us 20 parts of 37 per cent.

BASIC FUNDAMENTALS OF WATER CHEMISTRY

TABLE OF CONTENTS

	Page
Physical States of Matter	1
Chemical Change	1
Chemical Composition – Elements, Compounds and Atoms	1
Chemical Symbols, Formulae	3
Atomic Weight	3
Atomic Structure	4
Isotopes	5
Graphical Representation of Atomic Structure	5
Periodic Table of Elements	9
Valence and Atomic Structure	10
Valence and Chemical Combination—Valence Number	11
Laws of Chemistry	11
Molecules, Molecular Weight	12
Equations	12
Chemical Calculations	12
Ionization	14
Radicals	15
Equilibrium	15
Acids, Bases and Salts	15
pH Value	16
Equivalents of Acids and Bases	17
Neutralization of Acids and Bases	18
Indicators – Titration	18
Solutions	18
Organic Chemistry	21

BASIC FUNDAMENTALS OF WATER CHEMISTRY

Water treatment plant operators must have some knowledge of science, especially chemistry, to understand and control the water purification processes used in their plants. Fortunately a normal individual gains considerable knowledge of science during his lifetime. He observes material things and acquires through his personal experiences as well as through instruction by others a mass of information regarding their chemical and physical properties although he may not classify his knowledge on a scientific basis. The purpose of this chapter is to help a water plant operator to organize his present knowledge of chemistry and to add to it for the purpose of improving his understanding of water plant practices.

Physical States of Matter

All matter exists in one or more of three physical states: a) solid, b) liquid and c) gas. Some matter, water for example, can exist in all three physical states. Thus water may be solid (as ice), liquid (as ordinary water), or gas (as water vapor). Many times the transition from one physical state to another may be brought about by applying or taking away heat from the substance and this is true of water. It is not true of all matter, however, since an attempt to do so may have no appreciable effect or may bring about a different kind of change in the substance - a chemical change.

Chemical Change

Suppose we attempt to make a piece of wood become liquid by heating it, just as we can make a piece of ice liquid by heating it. We would soon find that heat does not liquify wood but chars it and, if enough heat is applied, burns it. We cannot by any means at our disposal restore the wood to its original state after it is burned as we could the original ice by refreezing the water. Excessive heat has produced a fundamental and irreversible change in the composition of the wood. This is an example of a chemical change—an alteration of both composition and properties of a substance.

Chemical Composition—Elements, Compounds and Atoms

Centuries of study have brought to man the knowledge that all of the many kinds of matter in this universe are composed of at least 114 basic substances which chemists call "elements." Some elements such as iron, copper, silver, gold and carbon, are well-known to everyone while others are so rare that they were isolated only recently after long years of effort. All materials are made of these elements existing alone or in combination as "chemical compounds."

Table I

Elements of Importance in Water Chemistry

Element	Chemical Symbol	Atomic Weight	Atomic Number	Valence Number	Corresponding Equivalent Weight
Aluminum	Al	26.98	13	3	8.99
Calcium	Ca	40.08	20	2	20.04
Carbon	C	12.01	6	2	6
				4	3
Chlorine	Cl	35.45	17	1	35.45
				3	11.82
				5	7.09
				7	5.06
Copper	Cu	63.54	29	1	63.54
				2	31.77
Fluorine	F	19.00	9	1	19.00
Hydrogen	H	1.008	1	1	1.008
Iron	Fe	55.85	26	2	27.93
				3	18.62
Magnesium	Mg	24.31	12	2	12.16
Manganese	Mn	54.99	25	2	27.49
				3	18.33
				4	13.75
				6	9.17
				7	7.86
Nitrogen	N	14.01	7	3	4.67
				5	2.80
Oxygen	O	16.00	8	2	8.00
Phosphorus	P	30.98	15	3	10.33
				5	6.20
Potassium	K	39.10	19	1	39.10
Silicon	Si	28.09	14	4	7.02
Sodium	Na	22.99	11	1	22.99
Sulfur	S	32.06	16	2	16.03
				4	8.02
				6	5.34

A chemical element may be defined as a chemical substance which cannot be decomposed into simpler substances by *ordinary* chemical change. Water, a chemical compound, may be decomposed easily into hydrogen and oxygen which are chemical elements. It is not possible, however, to decompose hydrogen and oxygen into still simpler substances without altering their basic identity. Table I lists a number of elements of particular importance to water chemistry and includes data regarding their properties. In the paragraphs that follow the significance of these data will be discussed.

The smallest part of an element which can exist and retain all of the chemical properties associated with the element is called an "atom." If one attempts to break down an atom of an element into lighter fragments, he may succeed if he applies extraordinary techniques, but after the breakdown, he no longer has the same element. He will have an element of lighter weight plus a considerable amount of energy in the form of heat and light. This process, popularly called "atom-smashing," or fission, is the basis for atomic energy and is outside the scope of this chapter.

Chemical Symbols, Formulae

It is convenient to represent each of the elements by a "symbol" rather than writing out its name. Symbols are in effect a form of shorthand applied to chemistry. (See Table I, column 2). Students of chemistry quickly learn the symbols for the more common elements and thereafter seldom write out their full names.

A combination of symbols to indicate a chemical compound is called the "formula" for the compound. A formula not only indicates the elements in the compound but by means of subscript numerals the number of atoms of each element in the compound.

Examples:
Symbol for hydrogen — H
Symbol for oxygen — O
Formula for water — H_2O; signifying that the compound, water, has 2 atoms of hydrogen combined with 1 atom of oxygen. Note that single atoms have no subscript.
Symbol for sodium — Na
Symbol for chlorine — Cl
Formula for sodium chloride (ordinary salt) — NaCl; signifying that the compound, sodium chloride, has 1 atom of sodium combined with 1 atom of chlorine.
Symbol for iron — Fe
Symbol for oxygen — O
Formula for ferric oxide (red rust) Fe_2O_3; signifying the compound, ferric oxide, has 2 atoms of iron combined with 3 atoms of oxygen.
Chemical formulas for other compounds of particular interest to water plant operators are listed in Table V (See page 73).

Atomic Weight

Elements, being material things have "mass," meaning that they are acted upon by the force of gravity. A practical measure of mass is "weight." In chemistry, the masses of all substances are expressed in terms of the metric system, the basic weight unit of which is the "gram." Different elements have different masses and this property together with other physical and chemical properties helps to identify elements.

Because of the different weight systems in effect in various countries of the world, the weights of elements are always stated in relative terms. The weight of an atom of carbon (the basic unit) is designated as 12 and the atomic weights of all of the other elements are designated by values which express the relationship of the mass of an atom of the element to the mass of an atom of carbon. On this basis, the mass of an atom of oxygen (atomic weight) is 16. This means, $\dfrac{\text{weight of an atom of oxygen}}{\text{weight of an atom of carbon}} = \dfrac{16}{12}$ The lightest element, hydrogen, has the atomic weight 1.008 and the heaviest, mendelevium (Md) has an atomic weight of 256. The heaviest naturally occurring element is uranium with an atomic weight of 238. Column 3 of Table I lists the atomic weights of the elements in column 1.

Formula weight — The formula weight of a compound equals the sum of the atomic weights of of all of the atoms making up the compound.

Atomic Structure

It is not necessary to have detailed knowledge of atomic structure to work with chemicals and make use of chemical reactions; chemistry was already an old science when various theories of atomic structure were evolved. Properties of chemical elements can be understood more fully and the mechanisms of chemical reactions can be explained more clearly through a knowledge of atomic structure. Some of the simpler concepts of this subject are presented here.

It was stated earlier that an atom is the smallest part of an element which can exist and still retain all of the properties of the element. Just how small is an atom? It is much too small to be seen with even the most powerful microscopes. It has been estimated that 100 million atoms would be required to make a line one inch long, and yet, despite the difficulty of studying such small objects, much has been learned about them. We know, for example, that atoms are composed of still smaller particles. These include protons, neutrons, electrons, and perhaps others. When they are associated together in a unit, namely an atom, they confer upon it characteristic properties. When by use of extraordinary force they are dissociated from each other the properties of the atom are altered.

We also know that the components of an atom are arranged in a fashion similar to our solar system with protons and neutrons representing the sun and electrons representing the planets. Just as planets orbit about the sun as a nucleus of the solar system, electrons orbit about the atomic nucleus of protons and neutrons. In our solar system each planet rotates in an orbit of its own but this is not necessarily true of atoms for one or more electrons may occupy a single orbit or "shell"—the term preferred by atomic scientists.

Let us now consider in greater detail the various components of an atom.

A proton is a particle of matter located in the nucleus of the atom. It has a mass of 1.007594 with respect to the chemical standard of mass carbon with a mass of 12.01. The proton carries a single positive electrical charge.

A neutron is also a nuclear particle. Its mass is 1.008986, only slightly heavier than a proton. It does not bear an electrical charge.

An electron is an extremely small particle which rotates in a shell about the nucleus. The mass of an electron is so small (0.000549) that it is usually ignored when considering the weight of an atom. It carries a single negative electrical charge.

For an atom to be electrically neutral it must have as many positively charged protons in the nucleus as there are negatively charged electrons in the shells surrounding the neucleus. Since the neutrons in the nucleus do not bear any charges their number does not affect the electrical polarity of the atom.

The most fundamental fact regarding an atom is that its identity is established by the number of protons in the nucleus. This is known as its "atomic number" (Column 4, Table I) and in a neutral atom it also represents the number of electrons in the shells outside the nucleus. If, by use of extraordinary methods, a proton is dislodged from the nucleus of an atom, the identity of the atom is changed, that is, the original atom disappears and a new atom of a lower atomic number and lower mass is created. In the process of splitting protons from an atomic nucleus (nuclear fission) a tremendous amount of energy is released and this is the basis for atomic energy which was brought to the attention of everyone in 1945 by the atomic bomb. The bomb represented a massive release of energy from fissionable material in the form of elemental uranium. Peaceful use of atomic energy involves the *controlled* release of energy through *controlled* nuclear fission, a much more difficult process than exploding a bomb.

Isotopes

Loss of an electron from an atom does not change its identity nor does the loss of a neutron. Loss of an electron merely imparts a positive charge on the atom and loss of a neutron produces an atom of the same identity but smaller mass than the original. Such an atom is known as an "isotope". Most atoms have isotopes and many have several. Oxygen, for example, has 4 isotopes O^{16}, O^{17}, O^{18}, and O^{19}. All of the forms of oxygen have 8 protons but 8, 9, 10, and 11 neutrons respectively. Atomic weights ascribed to various elements represent the average weights of their isotopes, taking into account their relative abundance in the natural state.

Graphical Representation of Atomic Structure

The spatial relationship of orbital electrons and the nucleus of an atom is complex and pictorial representations are often used in an attempt to make it more comprehensible to students. Since the atom with electrons is a 3 dimensional entity, a better picture of its structure can be obtained with 3 dimensional models. These are available for lecture purposes but, of course, cannot help with printed texts. Figures 1 through 13 may serve in some degree, however, to clarify the subject. In these illustrations the nucleus is represented by a circle, and protons and neutrons in the nucleus are represented by their commonly used symbols, "p" for proton and "n" for neutron. A numeral adjacent to each of these symbols represents the number of protons and neutrons respectively present in the nucleus. Electrons are represented by the symbol e and their orbital paths or shells are represented by larger circles.

A sharp observer on studying figures 1.13 will note two important features:
1. The first shell outside the nucleus has a minimum of 1 electron and a maximum of 2 electrons.
2. The second shell outside the nucleus, if its exists, has a minimum of 1 electron and a maximum of 8 electrons.

Because of space limitations, it is not possible to illustrate all of the rules of atomic structure although additional ones should be mentioned.

ATOMIC MODELS

FIG. 1

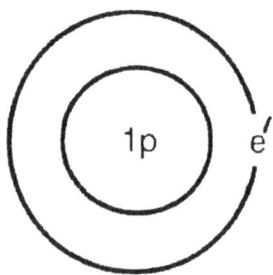

HYDROGEN (H)

FIG. 2

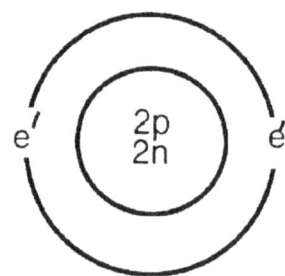

HELIUM (He)

FIG. 3

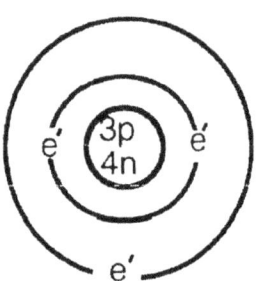

LITHIUM (Li)

FIG. 4

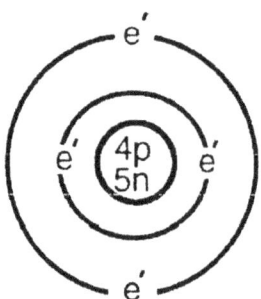

BERYLLIUM (Be)

FIG. 5

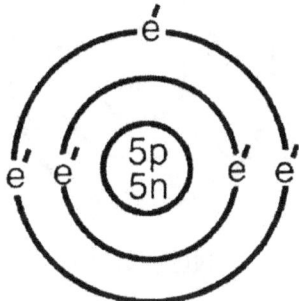

BORON (B)

FIG. 6

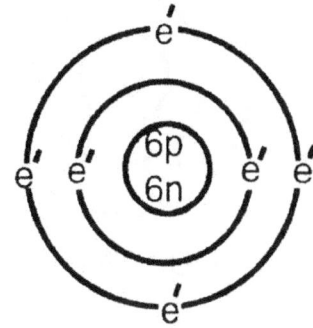

CARBON (C)

FIG. 7

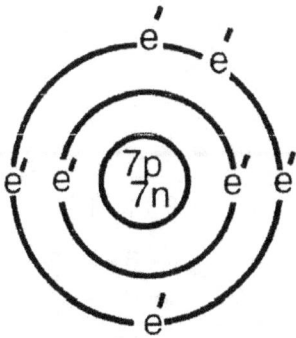

NITROGEN (N)

FIG. 8

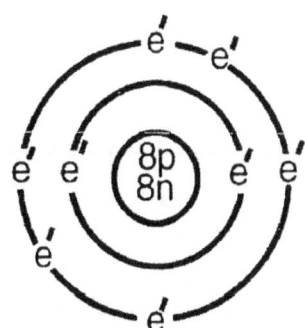

OXYGEN (O)

FIG. 9

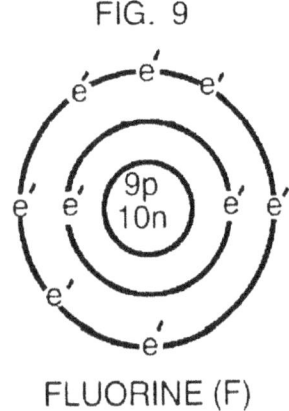

FLUORINE (F)

FIG. 10

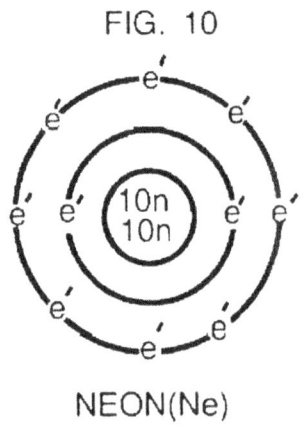

NEON (Ne)

FIG. 11

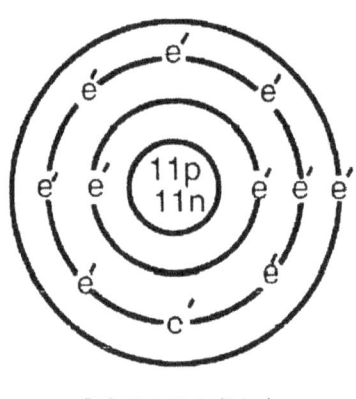

SODIUM (Na)

FIG. 12

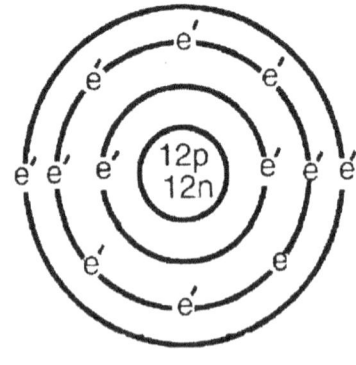

MAGNESIUM (Mg)

FIG. 13

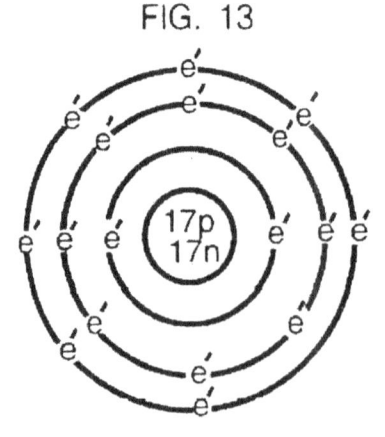

CHLORINE (Cl)

3. The first 18 elements have electrons arranged in orderly progression whereby the first shell holds a maximum of 2, the second shell a maximum of 8 and the third shell a maximum of 8 and no new shell is started until the one preceding it is filled.
4. Beyond the 18th element, however, this orderly progression no longer prevails and elements with 2 or more unfilled shells are common.
5. The maximum number of electrons which can occupy a shell is dependent upon its position with respect to the nucleus and can be calculated by the formula:

$$M = 2S^2$$

Where M = maximum number of electrons in the shell
S = the number of the shell with respect to the nucleus.
6. There are never more 8 electrons in the outermost shell.

On the basis of these rules, four distinct types of elements are recognized:
A. Those which have atoms with no unfilled electron shells. These are inert elements which do not combine with other elements.
B. Those which have atoms with 1 unfilled shell. These are "simple" elements.
C. Those which have atoms with 2 unfilled shells. These are "transition" elements.
D. Those which have atoms with 3 unfilled shells. These are "rare earth" elements.

Periodic Table of the Elements

Mendelejeff, a 19th century Russian chemist, noticed what he called "periodicity" of physical and chemical properties of the elements and he devised a table in which he grouped the known elements according to their properties. He left places for elements not then discovered but which he expected would be discovered later on the basis of periodicity. The table published in 1872 was subjected to many adjustments and rearrangements but its original basis remains grouping of elements with similar properties. An illustration of the modern table appears in Fig. 14. Vertical columns represent "Groups" of elements arranged on the basis of the number of electrons in their outer shells. Elements in Groups I through VII have 1 unfilled shell and therefore are classified as "simple" elements. Group I elements have only 1 electron inthe outer shell, Group II have 2 electrons, ect. Group VIII elements have completed shells of 8 electrons and are therefore in the "inert" class. Inertness is quite evidently associated with the lack of space to add on electrons from other atoms.

"Transition" electrons having 2 unfilled shells are grouped near the center of the periodic table. These also are arranged on the basis of similarity of properties but the relationship is not so definite as for the simple elements.

"Rare earth" elements each having 3 unfilled shells are arranged in 2 series in a separate table below the main table.

The horizontal arrangement of the elements also has significance. All of the elements on a single horizontal level (a single period) have the same number of atomic shells. There are, therefore, 7 periods with elements having from 1 to 7 shells of electrons in their atomic structure.

The periodic table was of great help to early chemists in studying chemical properties of the elements and especially helpful in predicting properties of elements not isolated at that time. Students of chemistry still can learn much by study of the periodic table.

FIG 14

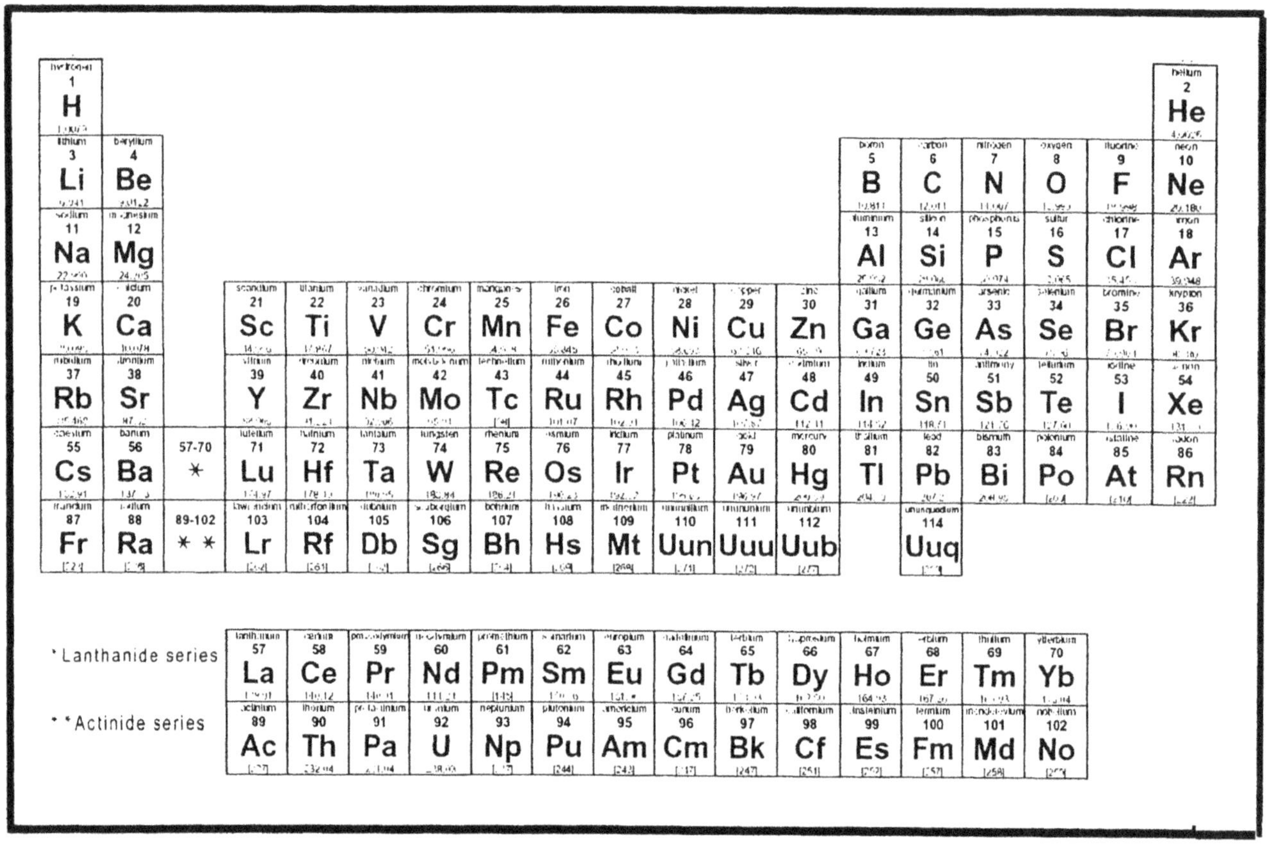

[Periodic Table of Elements]

PERIODIC TABLE OF ELEMENTS

Valence and Atomic Structure

Valence is a term synonymous with "combining power." One may say it is the relative "worth" of an atom of an element in combining with atoms of other elements to form compounds. It is expressed in small whole numbers ranging from 0 to 7 and these numbers may be either positive or negative. Loss of 1 electron from the outermost electron shell confers positive valence of 1 upon an atom; similarly, loss of 2 electrons confers positive valence of 2. Gain of electrons in the outermost shell confers negative valence. Referring to the periodic table (Figure 14), atoms of elements in Groups I, II, and III tend to lose electrons and therefore tend to become positively charged atoms since loss of an electron results in an excess of positively charged protons over negatively charged electrons.

Atoms of elements in Groups IV, V, VI, and VII tend to gain electrons and therefore tend to become negatively charged. It follows that positively charged atoms of Groups I, II, and III attract and are attracted to negatively charged atoms of Groups V through VII resulting in formation of electrically neutral chemical compounds. Sharing of electrons in this manner is known as covalence and is the basis for formation of all chemical compounds.

Unexplained as yet is the question as to why elements of Groups I, II, and III tend to lose electrons and elements of Groups IV through VII tend to gain electrons. The explanation is suggested by the arrangement of the electrons in the outermost shell of these elements. The most stable situation is where the outermost shell has 8 electrons. Group VIII elements are of this type. The tendency for atoms to lose electrons varies in this order: Group I, Group II, Group III, and the tendency for atoms to gain electrons varies in this order: Group VII, Group VI, Group V and Group IV. The strongest tendency toward combination lies, therefore, in those atoms which are furthest from the center of the periodic table. It will be noted on study of the table that this is associated with the number of atoms in the outermost shells. Atoms of Group I elements have a very strong tendency to lose electrons to atoms of Group VII elements because loss of the lone electron in the outermost shell of a Group I atom gives it a more stable configuration and gain of a single electron by an atom of a Group VII element completes its full complement of eight and thus gives it a more stable configuration.

There are other more complex aspects of valence than those outlined here but these must be left to more complete chemical texts.

Valence and Chemical Combination-Valence Number

The "valence number" of an element is the number of electrons of the element associated with formation of a particular compound. Since this number may be different for different compounds of an element, it follows, that elements may have more than one valence number. This fact frequently is difficult for students to understand. To illustrate the point, let us consider the element iron (Fe). Iron combines with oxygen to form 2 different compounds: FeO, a black colored oxide and Fe_2O_3, a red colored oxide. Red iron oxide (rust) is familiar to everyone, black oxide of iron is frequently observed in water plants particularly underneath the scale of cor-roded pipe. Iron also forms numerous compounds with other elements in which it may have a valence number 2 or a valence number 3. Many other elements also have more than one valence number depending upon the chemical compounds involved. Since no one can remember all of the facts, such as these, regarding the various elements and compounds, chemists make frequent use of reference works which present these facts in tabular form.

Laws of Chemistry

Over many years of observation some relationships in the field of chemistry seem to prevail without deviation and, because of this, these have become known as "laws." It is appropriate at this time that some of these be set down so that the reader may be aware of them.

"The Law of Conservation of Matter" was one of the first to be recognized by early chemists. It may be stated in various ways. One of the simplest is "Matter can neither be created nor destroyed in a chemical reaction; it can only be changed from one form to another."

"The Law of Definite Proportions" states that "when a given compound is formed by the combination of elements the proportions, by weight, of the element making up the compound are always the same regardless of the mode of formation of the compound." Thus the proportion, by weight, of hydrogen to oxygen in the compound water (H_2O) is always the same regardless of the source of the water or the manner of its formation.

"The Law of Multiple Proportions"–If 2 or more compounds are composed of the same elements, the different weights of one element which combine with a fixed weight of another stand to each other in the ratio of small whole numbers. We can illustrate this by the compounds water (H_2O) and hydrogen peroxide (H_2O_2). Two atoms of hydrogen are found in both compounds but the number of atoms of oxygen and therefore the weight of oxygen found in hydrogen peroxide is exactly twice the amount found in water. The weight ratio is expressed:

$$\frac{\text{Wt. of oxygen in } H_2O}{\text{Wt. of oxygen in } H_2O_2} = 1/2$$

"The Law of Combining Weight"–In every compound the proportions by weight of each element may be expressed by a definite number (atomic weight) or an integral multiple of that number. This law is essentially an extension of the law of multiple proportions wherein the basic weight of an element (i.e., atomic weight) is included in the statement.

All chemists make use of the principles of chemical measurement through these laws. They enable them to determine the amounts of various elements and compounds required to react with definite amounts of other elements and compounds. It enables them, in short, to make practical use of the science of chemistry.

Molecules, Molecular Weight

Earlier we defined an atom as the smallest part of an element which can exist and retain all of the chemical properties associated with that element. We can now define another unit, "the molecule" as the smallest unit of a compound. Molecular weight of the compound, it follows, is the sum of the atomic weights of the atoms composing the compound.

Equations

A chemical equation is an expression made up of chemical formulae to indicate chemical changes (reactions) which take place when these substances are brought together. For example, we can illustrate what happens when calcium carbonate ($CaCO_3$) is brought into contact with sulfuric acid (H_2SO_4) by writing an equation, $CaCO_3 + H_2SO_4 \rightarrow CaSO_4 + H_2CO_3$. This equation tells us that a reaction takes place and the products of the reaction are calcium sulfate and carbonic acid.

Similarly we can write an equation to illustrate the rusting of iron, $Fe + O_2 \rightarrow Fe_2O_3$. Iron and oyxgen combine to produce iron oxide (rust). In this case the equation as written violates the law of conservation of matter which states that matter cannot be created or destroyed. The violation in this case is the increase of 1 atom of iron on the left side of the equation to 2 atoms on the right side and the increase of 2 atoms of oxygen on the left side to 3 atoms on the right side. We could avoid this by writing the equation $2Fe + 3O \rightarrow Fe_2O_3$, but this is not correct either because gaseous oxygen exists as O_2 not O. To make the equation conform to the facts, we should write it as follows: $4Fe + 3O_2 \rightarrow 2Fe_2O_3$. This process is known as "balancing" an equation. Balancing of simple equations is easily accomplished by inspection. Balancing of complex equations involving a number of reactants and products may be quite difficult. A most important prerequisite for balancing any equation is that the identity of all of the reactants and products be known and their formulas be recorded correctly.

Chemical Calculations

Chemists make practical use of equations to calculate the amounts of reactants required to produce desired amounts of products, to determine the amount of one reactant required to match a. given amount of another reactant, and for similar purposes. To illustrate the method, let us consider again the equation for rusting of iron by oxygen:

$$4Fe + 3O_2 \rightarrow 2Fe_2O_3$$

From Table I, we determine the atomic weight of iron is 55.85 and the atomic weight of oxygen is 16. Then 4 atoms of iron (Fe) are equivalent to 4 X 55.85 = 230.40. A molecule of oxygen contains 2 atoms of O (2 X 16.0) and 3 molecules of oxygen are equivalent to 3 X 2 X 16.0 = 96.0. A molecule of iron oxide is equivalent to 2 X 55.85 (the weight of 2 atoms of iron) plus 3 X 16.0 (the weight of 3 atoms of oxygen), a total of 111:70 + 48.0 = 159.70. Two such molecules of iron oxide then equals 2 X 159.70=319.40. The calculation corresponding to the equation is therefore:

$$4Fe + 3O_2 \rightarrow 2Fe_2O_3$$

4 X 55.85 + 3 X 16.0 X 2 = 2 X 55.85 X 2 + 3 X 16.0
223.40 + 96.0 = 319.40

Thus we know the 223.40 parts by weight of iron react with 96.0 parts by weight of oxygen to yield 319.40 parts by weight of iron oxide. Weight units may be anything, grams, pounds or tons, etc., but, of course, the unit chosen must be used consistently for all of the reactants and products of the reaction.

Equations and calculations of this kind are of great value to all who work with chemical processes including water plant operators. Suppose, for example, a water plant operator wishes to know the amount of alkalinity present in the water he is treating. The alkalinity of the water has influence on the coagulation process and it is desirable that its measure be known so that the amount of coagulants added may be sufficient but not excessive. Alkalinity is measured by reacting those chemicals in the water which are associated with alkalinity with a standard solution of sulfuric acid, that is, a solution of sulfuric acid in water made up to a definite concentration. The standard solution used for this purpose is one which has 0.9806 gram of H_2SO_4 in every 1,000 ml of the solution, that is 0.9806 mg of acid per ml of solution. Using a process called titration, (to be explained later), the exact amount of acid solution required to react with the alkalinity in 100 ml of the water sample, is determined. Let us suppose that it is 25.0 ml. We can now calculate the amount of calcium carbonate (alkalinity) in the water sample using as a basis the reaction between sulfuric acid and calcium carbonate. Thus:

$$CaCO_3 + H_2SO_4 \rightarrow CaSO_4 + H_2CO_3$$

Referring to Table III where the atomic weights of all of the elements involved in this equation are given we find:

$$CaCO_3 = \underset{40.08}{Ca} + \underset{12.01}{C} + \underset{3 \times 16.00}{O_3} = 100.9$$

$$H_2SO_4 = \underset{2 \times 1.01}{H_2} + \underset{32.06}{S} + \underset{4 \times 16.00}{O_4} = 98.06$$

$$CaSO_4 = \underset{40.08}{Ca} + \underset{32.04}{S} + \underset{4 \times 16.00}{O_4} = 136.03$$

$$H_2CO_3 = \underset{2 \times 1.01}{H_2} + \underset{12.01}{C} + \underset{3 \times 16.00}{O_3} = 62.03$$

writing these values under the equation, we get

$$CaCO_3 + H_2SO_4 \rightarrow CaSO_4 + H_2CO_3$$

$$100.9 + 98.06 \rightarrow 136.12 + 62.03$$

Now 25 ml of standard H_2SO_4 solution contains 25.0 X 0.9806 mg of H_2SO_4 and 100 ml of water contains X mg of $CaCO_3$ and the following proportion expresses the relationship between these amounts

$$\frac{X}{100.09\,mg} = \frac{25 \times 0.9806\,mg}{98.06\,mg}$$ when the equation is solved we find that X = 25.01 mg in the 100 ml of sample.

If we wish to express this in terms of mg of $CaCO_3$ alkalinity per liter of sample (the usual practice) we multiply the result by ten (since one liter is ten times 100 ml.)

Thus, $\frac{25\,mg}{100\,ml} \times 10 = 250$ mg/liter, alkalinity.

Equations commonly used in water plants for purposes of calculation are:

$Cl_2 + H_2O \rightarrow HCl + HOCl$

$Ca(OCl)_2 + Na_2CO_3 \rightarrow 2NaOCl + CaCO_3$

$Al_2(SO_4)_3 + 3CaCO_3 + 3H_2O \rightarrow Al_2(OH)_6 + 3CaSO_4 + 3CO_2$

$CO_2 + H_2O \rightarrow H_2CO_3$

$CaCO_3 + H_2CO_3 \rightarrow Ca(HCO_3)_2$

$Ca(HCO_3)_2 + Ca(OH)_2 \rightarrow 2CaCO_3 + 2H_2O$

$Ca(HCO_3)_2 + Na_2CO_3 \rightarrow CaCO_3 + 2NaHCO_3$

$NH_3 + HOCl \rightarrow NH_2Cl + H_2O$

$NH_2Cl + HOCl \rightarrow NHCl_2 + H_2O$

$NHCl_2 + HOCl \rightarrow NCl_3 + H_2O$

$CaCO_3 + H_2SO_4 \rightarrow CaSO_4 + H_2CO_3$

$Ca(HCO_3)_2 + H_2SO_4 \rightarrow CaSO_4 + 2H_2CO_3$

Ionization

Many elements combine with each other spontaneously on contact. This combination may take place slowly or rapidly and in some instances even explosively. Combinations of elements to form compounds are influenced by many factors such as heat, moisture, or catalytic agents-agents which promote a reaction but do not themselves undergo any change during the reaction. Most chemical reaction takes place in the presence of water because water has a property of splitting some molecules dissolved in it into positively and negatively charge atoms which are called "ions." The process of producing ions is called "ionization" and a molecule which produces ions when dissolved in water is said to "ionize" or "dissociate into ions." Ionization is illustrated graphically as an equation, thus

$NaCl \rightarrow Na^+ + Cl^-$

The charged atoms are called ions.

Positively charged ions are designated "cations" and negatively charged ions are designated "anions." The charges must be equal in magnitude and opposite in sign, otherwise the solution itself would have a charge and this is not the case.

When a molecule dissociates in water, the charges must be such that they equalize even when there are more atoms of one kind than another in the molecule. Example, ferric chloride ($FeCl_3$) ionizes as follows:

$FeCl_3 \rightarrow Fe^{+++} + 3Cl^-$

15

Radicals

Some molecules dissociate or ionize to yield groups of atoms, positively charged cations or negatively charged anions. Ammonium chloride (NH_4Cl) ionizes, $NH_4Cl \rightarrow (NH_4)^+ + Cl^-$ where $(NH_4)+$ is ammonium cation and $Cl-$ is chloride anion. Another example, sodium sulfate (Na_2SO_4) ionizes, $Na_2SO_4 \rightarrow 2Na^+ + (SO_4)^{--}$. In this instance there are two sodium cations and one sulfate anion. Combinations of atoms acting as a unit, such as $(NH_4)+$ and $(SO_4)^{--}$ are called "radicals."

Equilibrium

In writing equations to illustrate a reaction an arrow is often used to indicate the course of the reaction. Sometimes, however, 2 arrows ($\rightleftarrows$) or an equal sign (=) are used and this practice is probably more correct because not all reactions progress to the point where there is complete disappearance of the reactants. In most cases there is a state of equilibrium where reactants and products are present simultaneously. This state of equilibrium is best illustrated in an equation as a double arrow ($\rightleftarrows$). An equilibrium state may be shifted in one direction or another by physical and chemical factors such as heat, acidity, alkalinity or physical removal of one of the products. Chemical manufacturing processes are designed to take advantage of such factors to increase the yield of a desired product and to suppress the yield of an undesired product. Chemical equilibrium is attained also in ionization. Not all substances which dissolve in water ionize, however, and many ionize only to a very slight degree. In the following paragraphs we will discuss various types of substances in relation to ionization.

Acids, Bases, and Salts

An "acid" is a substance which yields $H+$ ions when it dissociates in water. Some examples:

HCl (hydrochloric acid) ($\rightleftarrows$) $H^+ + Cl^-$. This is an acid which ionizes almost completely and for that reason it is considered a very strong acid. Referring: to an acid as "strong" is another way of saying it yields a high concentration of hydrogen ions.

H_2S (hydrogen sulfide) ($\rightleftarrows$) $2H^+ + S^{--}$. This is a very weak acid because its degree of ionization is very low.

Hydrochloric (HCl), nitric (HNO_3) and sulfuric (H_2SO_4) are among the strongest acids and carbonic (H_2CO_3), boric (H_3BO_4) and hydrosulfuric, another name for hydrogen sulfide (H_2S) are among the weakest acids. There are many others which are intermediate between these extremes.

A "base" is a substance which yields hydroxyl $(OH)^-$ ions when it dissociates in water.

A base which yields a high concentration of hydroxyl ions is a "strong" base and one which yields a low concentration of hydroxyl ions is a "weak" base.

Examples: $NaOH \rightleftarrows Na^+ + (OH)^-$ a strong base

$Ca(OH)_2 \rightleftarrows Ca^{++} + 2(OH)^-$ a weak base

$Fe(OH)_3 \rightleftarrows Fe^{+++} + 3(OH)^-$ a weak base

"Salts" ordinarily yield neither hydrogen nor hydroxyl ions. Sodium chloride dissociates as follows: NaCl $\rightleftarrows$ Na+ + Cl-. Since neither H$^+$ or OH$^-$ ions are produced, NaCl is a neutral salt neither acid or alkaline. Other salts which are products of a reaction between a strong acid and a weak base, such as aluminum sulfate $Al_2(SO_4)_3$ are acidic because when they ionize a secondary reaction takes place as follows:

$Al_2(SO_4)_3 \rightarrow 2Al^{+++} + 3(SO_4)^{--}$

$H_2O \rightleftarrows H^- + (OH)^-$

$2Al^{+++} + 3H + OH^- \rightleftarrows Al(OH)_3 + 3H^+$

$Al(OH)_3$ is not ionized as much as water itself and therefore aluminum ions remove hydroxyl ions from water to form an undissolved solid thus leaving an excess of H$^+$ ions in solution. There is no tendency for H$^+$ ions to combine with $(SO_4)^{--}$ because H_2SO_4 almost completely dissociates. The phenomenon illustrated above where a salt reacts with water, is called "hydrolysis." A similar but converse situation prevails with salts formed from a weak acid and a strong base. Sodium carbonate is an alkaline salt because of ionization, carbonate ions $(CO_3)^{--}$ tend to remove H$^+$ ions from solution by forming very slightly ionized carbonic acid and thus leaving an excess of (OH)$^-$ ions present in the solution.

A few salts such as mercuric chloride ($HgCl_2$) do not ionize appreciably even though they are slightly soluble in water. They are exceptions to the general rule, however.

pH Value

As mentioned previously, water ionizes to a slight degree producing both hydrogen and hydroxyl ions:

$H_2O \rightleftarrows H^+ + (OH)^-$

It may be said that water is both an acid and a base because it produces both hydrogen and hydroxyl ions. Since these are present in identical concentrations, however, water is considered neutral. It is known that water ionizes to the extent that the concentration of each of the ions, H$^+$ and (OH)$^-$, is $\frac{1 \text{ molecular weight}}{10,000,000}$ per liter.

A short mathematical way of writing this concentration is $\frac{1}{10^7}$ M (molecular weights per liter) or, still shorter, 1×10^{-7} M (molar, a term discussed later in this chapter). This is a very small number and chemists, like most people, prefer to use numbers which are easier to comprehend. The term "pH" was suggested to designate hydrogen, ion concentration and the term was defined as "the logarithm of the reciprocal of the hydrogen ion concentration."

Thus hydrogen ion concentration = $\frac{1}{10^7}$ Molar, the reciprocal of the hydrogen ion concentration = 1×10^7 and the logarithm of the reciprocal of the hydrogen ion concentration (pH)=7.0. Since, as we noted previously, in pure water the hydrogen ion concentration equals the hydroxyl ion concentration $_p$(OH) also equals 7.0. From a chemical law, called "The Law of Mass Action", we know that whenever water is present H$^+$ X (OH)$^-$ = a constant value = 1×10^{-14}, or, in other words pH+p(OH) =14.

It is not necessary, therefore, for us to determine both pH and p(OH); all we need to do if p(OH) is desired is measure pH (with an instrument designed for the purpose) and subtract the value from 14. There are several water treatment processes, notably chlorination and coagulation, which are affected by pH of the water. These will be discussed in later chapters of this manual.

The pH scale. Table II lists the hydrogen ion concentrations in terms of molecular weight in grams per liter of solution versus the corresponding pH.

Table II

A gram molecular weight Of H+ ions per liter (M)	B reciprocal of A	C Log B (pH)	
1.0	1.0	0	
0.1	10	1	
0.01	100	2	
0.001	1,000	3	Acid
0.0001	10,000	4	
0.00001	100,000	5	
0.000001	1,000,000	6	
0.0000001	10,000,000	7	(neutrality)
0.00000001	100,000,000	8	
0.000000001	1,000,000,000	9	
0.0000000001	10,000,000,000	10	Alkaline
0.00000000001	100,000,000,000	11	
0.000000000001	1,000,000,000,000	12	
0.0000000000001	10,000,000,000,000	13	
0.00000000000001	100,000,000,000,000	14	

Careful examination of this table discloses several important facts
1. When the hydrogen ion concentration is highest, pH is lowest.
2. When the hydrogen ion concentration is lowest, pH is highest.
3. Neutrality at pH 7 is midpoint in the scale; pH values lower than 7 represent higher hydrogen ion concentration (more acid) than neutrality and pH values higher than 7 represent lower hydrogen ion concentrations (more alka-line) than neutrality.
4. pH values between the values listed in column C represent hydrogen concentration lying between those listed in column A and column B. For example, pH 5.5 represents a H⁻ ion concentration of 0.00000316 gram molecular weight/liter (3.16×10^{-6} gram molecular weight/liter). The value 0.00000316 would appear in column A and the corresponding value in column B is 316,000.

Equivalents of Acids and Bases

An equivalent weight of an acid is the weight of an acid which will supply one gram molecular weight of H+ ions (1.0 gram) in a liter of a solution of the acid in water. For acids which ionize to produce one H^+ ion per molecule of the acid, an equivalent weight of the acid is the same as its molecular weight. These are called "monoacids." These acids which produce 2H+ ions per molecule of the acid (example, $H_2SO_4 \rightarrow 2H^+ + (SO_4)^{--}$) are called "diacids" and those acids which produce $3H^+$ ions per molecule example $H_3PO_4 \rightarrow 3H^+ + (PO_4)^{---}$) are called "triacids."

It follows that an equivalent weight of a monoacid is equal to the molecular weight of the acid in grams, an equivalent weight of a diacid is equal to 1/2 of the molecular weight of the acid in grams and an equivalent weight of a triacid is equal to 1/3 of the molecular weight of the acid in grams.

A similar situation exists with respect to bases. A "monobase" produces an equivalent weight of hydroxyl ions (17 grams) when one molecular weight of it is present in water solution; a dibase produces an equivalent weight of hydroxyl ions when 1/2 of the molecular weight of the substance is present in one liter of water solution and a tribase produces an equivalent weight of hydroxyl ions when 1/3 of the molecular weight of the substance is present in one liter of water solution.

The term "equivalent" is not restricted to acids and bases. A further discussion of its significance will be found under *Solutions*.

Neutralization of Acids and Bases

Consider what happens when an acid solution and an alkaline solution each containing one equivalent of hydrogen ions and hydroxyl ions respectively, are mixed:

$HCl \rightleftarrows H^+ + Cl^-$ acid

$NaOH \rightleftarrows Na^+ + (OH)^-$ base

The H^+ ions and the $(OH)^-$ ions combine to form water which is only slightly ionized. The effect is to remove H + and $(OH)^-$ from the system until they are almost all gone. When the reaction is completed the only H^+ and $(OH)^-$ ions left are the insignificant concentration obtained from ionization of water. There are, of course, free Na^+ and Cl^- ions present in abundance because NaCl is a highly ionizable salt. This type of reaction involving acids and bases is called "neutralization" and is very common in chemistry.

Indicators Titration

An indicator is a substance which changes color according to conditions which prevail in a reaction system. In the mutual neutralization of HCl and NaOH described above, an indicator of the proper type would indicate by a sharp color change the instant neutrality is attained. If one solution is added in increments of small volume to the other solution containing the indicator a sharp color change at the attainment of neutrality enables the chemist to exactly match the two solutions. This process is called "titration" and a more detailed discussion of it will follow later in this chapter. The indicators used for acid-base titrations are sensitive to pH and a very slight shift of pH at the point of neutrality brings about a striking change in color of the solution even though the amount of indicator added is usually very small. There are many indicators used in chemistry and some of them are sensitive to reactions other than pH change. Among these are oxidation-reduction indicators and indicators which form colored compounds on chemical combination with a reactant or a product of a reaction.

Solutions

Since most chemical reactions take place while the reactants are in solution, it is important that facts pertaining to solutions and their properties be well understood.

A solution is made up of 2 or more components. One component is the "solvent" which dissolves the other component or components, each of which is called a "solute." Both the solvent and the solute may be in various physical states, that is solid, liquid, or gaseous. For example, we may have a solution of a solid in a liquid, a gas in a liquid, a solid in a solid, and other combinations. It is also possible to have a combination of more than one solute in a single solvent.

Some solutes are infinitely soluble in a solvent; ethyl alcohol, for example, is soluble in water in all proportions. These two substances may be said to be mutually soluble. Most solutes have only limited solubility in a solvent, however, and when the solubility limit is reached no more will be dissolved. The solvent and the excess solute exist then in two distinct phases which may be liquid-liquid, liquid-solid or liquid-gaseous.

Concentration of Solutions. There are a number of terms used with reference to concentration of solutions which must be understood.

A *concentrated solution* is one where the amount of solute in a given volume of solvent is relatively great.

A *dilute solution* is one where the amount of solute in a given volume of solvent is relatively small.

Obviously these two terms are not definite with respect to amount.

Percentage Concentration. More precise terminology is available for expressing the concentration of a solute in a solvent. "Percent concentration" is often expressed as the

$$\frac{\text{weight of the solute}}{\text{weight of the solvent}} \times 100.$$ This is a more accurate way of expressing concentration than the terms "concentrated" or "dilute" but it too is unsatis-factory from a practical standpoint because it is difficult to weigh large volumes of liquids. Frequently percent concentration is considered to mean $\frac{\text{weight of the solute in gram}}{100 \text{ ml of solvent}}$ This implies that 100 ml of any solvent weighs 100 grams- an unjustified assumption if accurate measure is desired. It is, however, a reasonably close approximation if water is the solvent.

Still another interpretation of "percent concentration" is possible

$$\frac{\text{weight of solution}}{\text{weight of solution}} \times 100.$$ This is the most accurate of the 3 definitions for percentage concentration but again it could become necessary to weigh large volumes of solution.

Molar Concentration., Because of the different definitions possible for "per cent concentrations" chemists have adopted the term "molar concentration" which means 1 mole of solute per liter of solution. A mole is 1 formula weight of solute in grams. Thus sodium chloride (NaCl) has the formula weight

Na + Cl = NaCl

22.99 g + 35.45 g = 58.54 g

A mole of sodium chloride, therefore, weighs 58.54 grams and a 1 molar solution of sodium chloride equals 58.54 g of sodium chloride per liter of solution *(not per liter of solvent)*. This is a very precise way of expressing concentration and suitable for most routine work. For the highest possible accuracy, however, the temperature of the solvent must be taken into account since liquids expand and contract as the temperature rises or falls. When making "standard" solutions a chemist adjusts the temperature to the level at which the solution will be used to avoid changes in concentration. Molar concentration is abbreviated "M"; thus a 1 molar solution is written 1 M.

Normal solution. Another way of expressing concentrations of solutions is in terms of normality. A "normal" solution is defined as a solution containing 1 "equivalent" per liter. The term "equivalent" was used before in discussion of acids and bases. For acids, one equivalent was described as the weight of an acid which would supply one gram molecular weight of H^+ ions (1.0008 grams) in a liter of solution of the acid in water. For bases, it was described as the weight of a base which would produce one gram molecular weight of $(OH)^-$ ions (17.008 grams) in a liter of a solution of the base in water. Such concentrations of acid and bases can also be called "normal" solutions for a "normal" solution is described as one which has 1 equivalent weight of the substance per liter of solution and by the same token all normal solutions are equivalent to each other. Normal concentration is abbreviated "N"; thus a 1 normal solution is written 1 N. In the discussion of acids and bases the term "equivalent" was introduced to explain the meaning of "mono", "di", and "tri" acids and bases. In the foregoing discussion of normality the term equivalent was also used to explain the meaning of normality.

It is important to understand that "equivalency" and "normality" do not refer to acids and bases alone or to ions alone but refer to salts as well as acids, unionized elements as well as ions and to compounds as well as elements. Both normality and equivalency are related to atomic weight and valence. Thus: equivalent weight of an element =

$$\frac{\text{atomic weight of the element}}{\text{valence of the element}}$$

Examples:

Equivalent weight of sodium (Na) = $\frac{22.997}{1} = 22.997$

Equivalent weight of calcium (Ca) = $\frac{40.08}{2} = 20.04$

In the use of this expression it is important, to note that valence of an element is not always the same. Copper (Cu) has an equivalent weight of 63.57 in the "cuprous" state where the valence is 1, but in the "cupric" state where its valence is 2, it has an equivalent weight of 31.785.

Equivalent weight of a compound = $\frac{\text{molecular weight of the compound}}{\text{total positive valence of compound}}$

Examples:
Equivalent weight of barium chloride ($BaCl_2$) =

$$\frac{137.36 + 2 \times 35.457}{2} = \frac{137.36 + 70.914}{2} = 104.137$$

Equivalent weight of filter alum $Al_2(SO_4)_3 \cdot 12H_2O$ =

$$\frac{2 \times 26.97 + 3(32.06 + 4 \times 16) + 12(2 \times 1.008 + 16)}{3(\text{valence of Al}) \times 2(\text{no. of Al atoms})} =$$

$$\frac{53.94 + 3(32.06 + 64) + 12(2.016 + 32)}{6} =$$

$$\frac{53.94 + 3 \times 96.06 + 12 \times 18.016}{6} =$$

$$\frac{53.94 + 288.18 + 216.192}{6} = \frac{558.312}{6} = 93.052$$

Equivalent weight of cupric chloride ($CuCl_2$) =

$$\frac{63.57 + 2 \times 35.457}{2} = \frac{63.57 + 70.914}{2} = \frac{134.484}{2} = 67.242$$

Equivalent weight of cuprous chloride (CuCl) = $\frac{63.570 + 35.457}{1} = 99.027$

Standard solutions. a standard solution is a solution which is made so accurately that it can be used to determine the concentration of substances in other solutions provided there is reaction between them which proceeds to a definite endpoint detectible by an indicator for example a standard solution of an acid can be used to determine the concentration of a base and the base solution is then said to be "standardized against" the acid. The base solution can then be used to standardize other acids. In this manner concentrations of many solutions are measured and all of the measurements can be referred to the original standard acid which is called the "primary" standard.

Primary standards - To be useful as a primary standard a substance must meet certain requirements which insure its stability under all usual environmental conditions.
1. it must be chemically pure
2. it must be a solid at ordinary temperatures
3. it must not readily absorb water from the air
4. it must not decompose at ordinary drying temperatures of 100-110° C

The United States Bureau of Standards have available a number of chemical compounds which meet these requirements and they can be purchased directly from the Bureau. Laboratory supply houses also supply primary standard chemicals for various purposes. These are listed in reagent catalogs issued by the individual firms.

Titration–a technique known as tritration is used to match an unknown reagent to a standard reageant. In addition to the two solutions, an appropriate indicator to detect the enpoint of the reaction between them, a beaker, a stirring rod, a burette, and a support for the burette are required. A burette is a glass tube open at the top and fitted with a stopcock on the lower end. The tube is graduated to measure accurately the volume (in milliliters) of the standard solution placed in it. The beaker contains an accurately measured volume of the solution to be assayed. One or two drops of the indicator are added to the beaker and while the liquid in the beaker is continuously stirred the standard solution is added in small increments. As the reaction progresses with each addition the amount of excess reagent in the beaker becomes smaller and its eventual exhaustion will be apparent by a sharp color change of the indicator: there is a direct relationship between the volume of standard solution used and the volume and concentration of the unknown solution in the beaker. For titrations involving normality this relationship is expressed:

volume of standard X normality of standard =
volume of unknown X normality of unknown

Transposing terms, we find normality of unknown =

$$\frac{\text{volume of standard} \times \text{normality of standard}}{\text{volume of unknown}}$$

The technique of titration is used extensively in water chemistry. Determinations of chloride, hardness, alkalinity, oxygen consumed value, chemical oxygen demand and biochemical oxygen demand all depend upon a titration procedure in the analytical method. More detailed information on this subject is given in the chapter "Laboratory Procedures."

Organic Chemistry

This is a specific branch of chemistry concerned with compounds of carbon. Carbon is unique among all other elements not only because its reactivity is great but also because of its ability to combine with itself in various ways to form a very large number of compounds. Many of the compounds of carbon were first isolated from living i.e. "organic" materials. It soon became apparent that all plant and animal tissue is composed of numerous carbon atoms in combination chiefly with hydrogen and oxygen but also to a much lesser degree with nitrogen, phosphorous, sulfur and metals.

Carbon has a valence of 4 and it is usually represented graphically as $-\overset{|}{\underset{|}{C}}-$.

The valence bonds shown must be shared with other atoms or groups of atoms for a stable structure. This can be done in various ways.

Examples:

```
    H   H   H   H
    |   |   |   |
H − C − C − C − C − H
    |   |   |   |
    H   H   H   H
         Butane
```
Carbon atoms in a straight chain. Here the 10 valence bonds are shared with hydrogen atoms to form the hydrocarbon butane- a well known combustible gas.

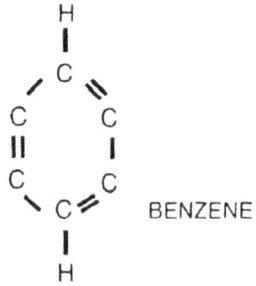

3-Methyl Pentane

Carbon atoms in a branched chain forming the hydrocarbon 3 methyl pentane.

The $H-\overset{|}{\underset{H}{C}}-H$ group is called methyl and it is attached to the third carbon in a 5 membered chain.

Carbon atoms in a ring formation with 6 reactive valence bonds. This is known as the "benzene" ring because if the available reactive sites are occupied by hydrogen atoms, the resulting compound is benzene. Thus:

```
        H
        |
       C
      ∕  ∥
     C    C
     ∥    |
     C    C
      ╲  ∕
       C        BENZENE
       |
       H
```

These are but two representatives of many thousands of carbon compounds in existance. The possibilities for new combinations are almost endless and new organic compounds are constantly being made synthetically. Many of the natural organic substances, for example, chlorophyll the green coloring matter in plants are extremely complex materials, and organic chemists may spend years first determining their structure and many more years learning how to sythesize them from simpler compounds.

Some of the organic materials to be found in water have defied the best efforts of chemists to identify them. Recently developed instruments such as gas-liquid chromatographs, infra-red analyzers and mass spectrometers are important tools aiding the chemists in this work. Identification and measurement of the concentration of the many kinds of pollutants which enter our water courses is an essential part of water pollution control. With increasing population density and increased industrialization of our country the variety and quantity of materials natural and synthetic, organic and inorganic, which enter our water courses threatens the usefulness of these streams for drinking water sources, recreational use and even industrial purposes. The role of chemistry in preservation of our greatest natural resource, water, is all important.

Table III

Chemicals Associated with Water Quality and Water Treatment

Chemical Name	Common Name	Chemical Formula
Ammonia	Ammonia	NH_3 (Ammonia gas) NH_4OH (Ammonia solution)
Alminum sulfate	Filter alum	$Al_2(SO_4)_3 \cdot 14H_2O$
Calcium carbonate	Limestone	$CaCO_3$
Calcium bicarbonate	....	$Ca(HCO_3)_2$
Calcium hydroxide	Hydrated lime or slaked lime	$Ca(OH)_2$
Calcium oxide	Unslaked lime or quick lime	CaO
Chlorine	....	Cl_2
Chlorine dioxide	....	ClO_2
Copper sulfate	Blue vitriol	$CuSO_4 \cdot 5H_2O$
Ferric chloride	....	$FeCl_3 \cdot 6H_2O$
Hydrochloric acid	Muriatic acid	HCl
Sufuric acid	Oil of vitriol	H_2SO_4
Sodium chloride	Salt	$NaCl$
Sodium carbonate	Soda ash	Na_2CO_3
Sodium bicarbonate	Soda	$NaHCO_3$
Sodium hydroxide	Lye	$NaOH$
Sodium phosphate	....	$Na_3PO_4 \cdot 12H_2O$
Fluosilicic acid (hydrofluosilicic acid)	....	N_2SiF_6
Sodium fluosilicate	....	Na_2SiF_6
Sodium fluoride	....	NaF
Carbon	Activated carbon	C

GLOSSARY

Acre-foot. A unit quantity of water; an amount which would cover 1 acre to a depth of 1 foot; consists of 326,000 gallons.

Alum. A chemical substance that is gelatinous when wet, usually potassium aluminum sulfate, used in water treatment plants for settling out small particles of foreign matter.

Consumptive use. Use of water resulting in a large proportion of loss to the atmosphere by evapotranspiration. Irrigation is consumptive use.

Crumb. A unit or particle of soil composed of many small grains sticking together.

Cubic feet per second (cfs). A measure of discharge; the amount of water passing a given point, expressed as number of cubic feet in each second.

Discharge. Outflow; the flow of a stream, canal, or aquifer. One may also speak of the discharge of a canal or stream into a lake, river, or an ocean.

Divide, drainage divide (sometimes called *watershed*). The boundary between one drainage basin and another.

Domestic use. Water use in homes and on lawns, including use for laundry, washing cars, cooling, and swimming pools.

Draw. A tributary valley or coulee, that usually discharges water only after a rainstorm.

Evaporation. The process by which water is changed from a liquid to a gas or vapor.

Evapotranspiration. Water withdrawn from soil by evaporation and plant transpiration. This water is transmitted to the atmosphere as vapor.

Flood. Any relatively high stream flow overtopping the natural or artificial banks in any reach of a stream.

Flood plain. The lowland that borders a river, usually dry but subject to flooding when the stream overflows its banks.

Food chain. The dependence of one type of life on another, each in turn eating or absorbing the next organism in the chain. Grass is eaten by cow; cow is eaten by man. This food chain involves grass, cow, and man.

Head race. The pipe or chute by which water falls downward into the turbine of a power plant.

Humus. Organic matter in or on a soil; composed of partly or fully decomposed bits of plant tissue derived from plants on or in the soil, or from animal manure.

Hydrology. The science of the behavior of water in the atmosphere, on surface of the earth, and underground.

Infiltration. The flow of a fluid into a substance through pores or small openings. The common use of the word is to denote the flow of water into soil material.

Leaching. The removal in solution of the more soluble minerals by percolating waters.

Nonconsumptive use. Uses of water in which but a small part of the water is lost to the atmosphere by evapotranspiration or by being combined with a manufactured product. Nonconsumptive uses return to the stream or the ground approximately the same amount as diverted or used.

Permeability. The property of soil or rock to pass water through it. This depends not only on the volume of the openings and pores, but also on how these openings are connected one to another.

Reaction turbine. A type of water wheel in which water turns the blades of a rotor, which then drives an electrical generator or other machine.

Salts. Dissolved chemical substances in water; table salt (sodium chloride) is but one of many such compounds which are found in water.

Sediment. Fragmental mineral material transported or deposited by water or air.

Self-supplied industrial use. Water supply developed by an individual industry or factory for its own use.

Specific yield. The amount of water that can be obtained from the pores or cracks of a unit volume of soil or rock.

Structure (in soil). Relation of particles or groups of particles which impart to the whole soil a characteristic manner of breaking; some types are crumb structure, block structure, platy structure, columnar structure.

Transpiration. The process by which water vapor escapes from the living plant and enters the atmosphere.

Watershed or drainage area. An area from which water drains to a single point; in a natural basin, the area contributing flow to a given place or a given point on a stream.

Water table. The top of the zone of saturation in the ground.

Weathering. Decomposition, mechanical and chemical, of rock material under the influence of climatic factors of water, heat, and air.

Water Equivalents

1 cubic foot per second (cfs) = 450 gallons per minute, or 7 1/2 gallons per second

1 cfs for 1 day, or 1 cfs-day = about 2 acre feet

1 acre foot = 326,000 gallons

1 cubic foot weighs 62.4 pounds

1 cubic foot = 7 ½ gallons

1 gallon = 8.33 pounds

1 ton = 240 gallons

GLOSSARY OF SEWAGE TREATMENT TERMS
CONTENTS

	Page
Activated Sludge Process……………………Arrester, Flame	1
Bacteria……………………………….Burner, Waste Gas	2
Centrifuge………………………………………………Chlorine	3
Clarifier……………………………………………….Digestion	4
Dilution……………………………………………...Effluent	5
Ejector, Pneumatic…………………………………….. Floc	6
Flocculator……………………………………………..Grease	7
Grinder, Screenings……………………………….Impeller	8
Index, Sludge Volume………………………...………….Mold	9
Most Probable Number, (MPN)……………………... Period	10
pH…………………………………………………………….Pump	11
Purification……………………………………………….Rate	12
Reaeration…………..……………………….Sedimentation	13
Seeding, Sludge……………………………………..Sewer	14
Sewerage……………………………………….…....Solids	15
Squeegee…………………………………………....Treatment	16
Trap, Flame……………………….. …………….Zooglea	17

137

GLOSSARY OF SEWAGE TREATMENT TERMS

A

Activated Sludge Process.—See **Process, Activated Sludge.**
Acre-Foot.—A unit of volume used to express the amount of material in a trickling filter. A depth of one foot on an area of one acre is an acre-foot. Regardless of shape, 43,560 cubic feet is equivalent to one acre foot.
Adsorption.—The adherence of dissolved, colloidal, or finely divided solids on the surfaces of solid bodies with which they are brought into contact.
Aeration.—The bringing about of intimate contact between air and a liquid by one of the following methods: Spraying the liquid in the air; or by agitation of the liquid to promote surface absorption of air.
 Diffused Air.—Aeration produced in a liquid by air passed through a diffuser.
 Mechanical.— (1) The mixing, by mechanical means, of sewage and activated sludge, in the aeration tank of the activated sludge process, to bring fresh surfaces of liquid into contact with the atmosphere. (2) The introduction of atmospheric oxygen into a liquid by the mechanical action of paddle or spray mechanisms.
 Modified.—A modification of the activated sludge process in which a shortened period of aeration is employed with a reduced quantity of suspended solids in the mixed liquor.
 Paddle-Wheel.—The mechanical agitation of sewage in the aeration tanks of the activated sludge process by means of paddle wheels.
 Spiral Flow.—A method of diffusing air in an aeration tank of the activated sludge process, where, by means of properly designed baffles, and the proper location of diffusers, a spiral or helical movement is given to the air and the tank liquor.
 Stage.—Division of activated sludge treatment into stages with intermediate settling tanks and return of sludge in each stage.
 Step.—A procedure for adding increments of sewage along the line of flow in the aeration tanks of an activated sludge plant.
 Tapered.—The method of supplying varying amounts of air into the different parts of an aeration tank in the activated sludge process, more at the inlet, less near the outlet, and approximately proportional to the oxygen demand of the mixed liquor under aeration.
Algae.—Primitive plants, one or many-celled, usually aquatic and capable of elaborating their foodstuffs by photosynthesis.
Algicide.—Any substance which kills algae.
Alkaline.—Water or soils containing sufficient amounts of alkaline substances to raise the pH above 7.0, or to harm the growth of crops.
Alkalinity.—A term used to represent the content of carbonates, bicarbonates, hydroxides, and occasionally borates, silicates, and phosphates in water. It is expressed in parts per million of calcium carbonate.
Alum.—A common name for aluminum sulfate.
Arrester, Flame.—A safety device on a gas line which allows gas, but not a flame, to pass through.

B

Bacteria.—Primitive plants, generally free of pigment, which reproduce by dividing in one, two, or three planes. They occur as single cells, groups, chains, or filaments, and do not require light for their life processes. They may be grown by special culturing out of their native habitat.

Aerobic.—Bacteria which require free (elementary) oxygen for their growth.

Anaerobic.—Bacteria which grow in the absence of free oxygen and derive oxygen from breaking down complex substances.

Coli-Aerogenes.—See Bacteria, Coliform Group.

Coliform Group.—A group of bacteria, predominantly inhabitants of the intestine of man but also found on vegetation, including all aerobic and facultative anaerobic grain-negative, non-spore-forming bacilli that ferment lactose with gas formation. This group includes five tribes of which the very great majority are Eschericheae. The Eschericheae tribe comprises three genera and ten species, of which *Escherichia Coli* and *Aerobacter Aerogenes* are dominant. *The Escherichia Coli* are normal inhabitants of the intestine of man and all vertebrates whereas Aerobacter Aerogenes normally are found on grain and plants, and only to a varying degree in the intestine of man and animals. Formerly referred to as *B.Coli*, B.Coli group, *ColiAerogenes Group*.

Facultative Anaerobic.—Bacteria which can adapt themselves to growth in the presence, as well as in the absence, of uncombined oxygen.

Parasitic.—Bacteria which thrive on other living organisms.

Pathogenic.—Bacteria which can cause disease.

Saprophytic.—Bacteria which thrive upon dead organic matter.

Bacterial Count.—A measure of the concentration of bacteria.

Most Probable Number.—See Page 10.

Plate.—Number of colonies of bacteria grown on selected solid media at a given temperature and incubation period, usually expressed as the number of bacteria per milliliter of sample.

Bed, Sludge.—An area comprising natural or artificial layers of porous material upon which digested sewage sludge is dried by drainage and evaporation. A sludge bed may be opened to the atmosphere or covered usually with a greenhouse-type superstructure. Also called Sludge Drying Bed.

Biochemical.—Resulting from biologic growth or activity, and measured by or expressed in terms of the ensuing chemical change.

Biochemical Action.—Chemical changes resulting from the metabolism of living organisms.

Biochemical Oxygen Demand (BOD).—The quantity of oxygen utilized in the biochemical oxidation of organic matter in a specified time and at a specified temperature. It is not related to the oxygen requirements in chemical combustion, being determined entirely by the availability of the material as a biological food and by the amount of oxygen utilized by the microorganisms during oxidation.

Biochemical Oxygen Demand, Standard.—Biochemical oxygen demand as determined under standard laboratory procedure for five days at 20°C, usually expressed in parts per million.

Buffer.—The action of certain solutions in opposing a change of composition, especially of hydrogen-ion concentration.

Burner, Waste Gas.—A device in a sewage treatment plant for burning the waste gas from a sludge-digestion tank.

C

Centrifuge.—A mechanical device utilizing centrifugal force to separate solids from liquids or for separating liquid emulsions.

Chamber.—A general term applied to a space enclosed by walls or to a compartment, often prefixed by a descriptive word, such as "grit chamber," "screen chamber," "discharge chamber," or "flushing chamber," indicating its function.

Chloramines.—Compounds of organic amines or inorganic ammonia with chlorine.

Chloride of Lime.—Obsolete term; see Chlorinated Lime.

Chlorinated Lime.—A combination of slaked lime and chlorine gas (also termed Bleaching Powder, Chloride of Lime, Hypochlorite of Lime, etc.). When dissolved in water, it serves as a source of chlorine.

Chlorination.—The application of chlorine.

    Break-Point.—The application of chlorine to water, sewage or industrial wastes containing free ammonia to provide free residual chlorination.

    Post.—The application of chlorine to water, sewage, or industrial wastes subsequent to any treatment. The term refers only to a point of application.

    Pre.—The application of chlorine to water, sewage, or industrial wastes prior to any treatment. This term refers only to a point of application.

Chlorine.—An element, when uncombined, exists as a greenish yellow gas about 2.5 times as heavy as air. Under atmospheric pressure and at a temperature of $-30.1°F$ the gas becomes an amber liquid about 1.5 times as heavy as water. The chemical symbol of chlorine is Cl, UP atomic weight is 35.457, and its molecular weight is 70.914.

    Available.—A term used in rating chlorinated lime and hypochlorites as to their total oxidizing power.

    Combined Available Residual.—That portion of the total residual chlorine remaining in water, sewage, or industrial wastes at the end of a specified contact period, which will react chemically and biologically as chloramines, or organic chloramines.

    Demand.—The difference between the amount of chlorine added to water, sewage, or industrial wastes and the amount of residual chlorine remaining at the end of a specified contact period. The demand for any given water varies with the amount of chlorine applied, time of contact, and temperas pure.

    Dose.—The amount of chlorine applied to a liquid, usually expressed in parts per million, or pounds per million gallons.

    Free Available Residual.—That portion of the total residual chlorine remaining in water. sewage, or industrial wastes at the end of a specified contact period. which will react chemically and biologically as hypochlorous acid, hypochlorite ion, or molecular chlorine.

    Liquid.—An article of commerce. Chlorine gas is generally manufactured by the electrolysis of a solution of common salt. The gas is dried and purified and is then liquefied by a combination of compression and refrigeration. Liquid chlorine is shipped under pressure in steel containers.

    Residual.--The total amount of chlorine (combined and free available chlorine) remaining in water, sewage, or industrial wastes at the end of a specified contact period following chlorination.

    Test, Iodometric.—The determination of residual chlorine in water, sewage, or industrial wastes by adding potassium iodide and titrating the liberated iodine with a standard solution of sodium thiosulfate, using starch solution as a colorimetric indicator.

Test, Ortho-Tolidine.—The determination of residual chlorine in water, sewage, or industrial wastes, using ortho-tolidine reagent and colorimetric standards.

Clarifier.—See Tank, Sedimentation.

Coagulation.—(1) The agglomeration of colloidal or finely divided suspended matter by the addition to the liquid of an appropriate chemical coagulant, by biological processes, or by other means. (2) The process of adding a coagulant and the necessary reacting chemicals.

Coils, Digester.—A system of pipes for hot water or steam installed in a sludge-digestion tank for the purpose of heating the sludge.

Coli-Aerogenes, or Coliform Group.—See Bacteria, Coliform Group.

Collector, Grit.—A device placed in a grit chamber to convey deposited grit to one end of the chamber for removal.

    Scum.—A mechanical device for skimming and removing scum from the surface of settling tanks.

    Sludge.—A mechanical device for scraping the sludge on the bottom of a settling tank to a sump, from which it can be drawn by hydrostatic or mechanical action.

Colloids.—Finely divided solids which will not settle but may be removed by coagulation or biochemical action.

Comminution.—The process of screening sewage and cutting the screenings into particles sufficiently fine to pass through the screen openings.

Concentration, Hydrogen-Ion.—See pH.

Copperas.—A common name for ferrous sulfate.

Copperas, Chlorinated.—A solution of ferrous sulfate and ferric chloride produced by chlorinating a solution of ferrous sulfate.

Cross Connection.—In plumbing, a physical connection through which a supply of potable water could be contaminated, polluted, or infected. A physical connection between water supplies from different systems.

Cubic Foot per Second.—A unit of discharge for measurement of flowing liquid, equal to a flow of one cubic foot per second past a given section. Also called Second-Foot.

D

Decomposition of Sewage.—The breakdown of the organic matter in sewage through aerobic and anaerobic processes.

Denitrification.—The reduction of nitrates in solution by biochemical action.

Deoxygenation.—The depletion of the dissolved oxygen in a liquid. Under natural conditions associated with the biochemical oxidation of organic matter present.

Detritus.—The sand, grit, and other coarse material removed by differential sedimentation in a relatively short period of detention.

Diffuser.—A porous plate or tube through which air is forced and divided into minute bubbles for diffusion in liquids. Commonly made of carborundum, alundum, or silica sand.

Digester.—A tank in which the solids resulting from the sedimentation of sewage are stored for the purpose of permitting anaerobic decomposition to the point of rendering the product nonputrescible and inoffensive. Erroneously termed digestor.

Digestion.—The processes occurring in a digester.

    Mesophilic.—Digestion by biological action at or below 113°F.

    Separate Sludge.—The digestion of sludge in separate tanks in which it is placed after it has been allowed to settle in other tanks.

Single-Stage Sludge.—Sludge digestion limited to a single tank for the entire digestion period.

Stage.—The digestion of sludge progressively in several tanks arranged in series.

Thermophilic.—Digestion carried on at a temperature generally between 113°F and 145°F.

Dilution. — (1) A method of disposing of sewage, industrial waste, or sewage treatment plant effluent by discharging it into a stream or body of water. (2) The ratio of volume of flow of a stream to the total volume of sewage or sewage treatment, ant effluent discharged into it.

Disinfection.—The killing of the larger portion (but not necessarily all) of the harmful and objectional microorganisms in, or on, a medium by means of chemicals, heat, ultraviolet light, etc.

Distributor.—A device used to apply liquid to the surface of a filter or contact bed, of two general types, fixed o movable. The fixed type may consist of perforated pipes or notched troughs, sloping boards, or sprinkler nozzles. The movable type may consist of rotating disks or rotating, reciprocating, or traveling perforated pipes or troughs applying a spray, or a thin sheet of liquid.

Dosing Tank.—A tank into which raw or partly treated sewage is introduced and held until the desired quantity has been accumulated, after which it is discharged at such a rate as may be necessary for the subsequent treatment.

Dryer.—A device utilizing heat to remove water.

Flash.—A device for vaporizing water from partly dewatered and finely divided sludge through contact with a current of hot gas or superheated vapor. Included is a squirrel cage mill for separating the sludge cake into fine particles.

Rotary.—A long steel cylinder, slowly revolving, with its long axis slightly inclined, through which passes the material to be dried in hot air. The material passes through from inlet to outlet, tumbling about.

E

E. Coli.—(Escherichia Coli).—A species of genus Escherichia bacteria, normal inhabitant of the intestine of man and all vertebrates. This species is classified among the Coliform Group. See Bacteria, Coliform Group.

Efficiency.—The ratio of the actual performance of a device to the theoretically perfect performance usually expressed as a percentage.

Average.—The efficiency of a machine or mechanical device over the range of load through which the machine operates.

Filter.—The operating results from a filter as measured by various criteria such as percentage reduction in suspended matter, total solids, biochemical oxygen demand, bacteria, color, etc.

Pump.—The ratio of energy converted into useful work to the energy applied to the pump shaft, or the energy difference in the water at the discharge and suction nozzles divided by the energy input at the pump shaft.

Wire-to-Water.—The ratio of the mechanical output of a pump, to the electrical input at the meter.

Effluent.—(1) A liquid which flows out of a containing space. (2) Sewage, water, or other liquid, partially or completely treated, or in its natural state, as the case may be, flowing out of a reservoir, basin, or treatment plant, or part thereof.

Final.—The effluent from the final unit of a sewage treatment plant.

Stable.—A treated sewage which contains enough oxygen to satisfy its oxygen demand.

Ejector, Pneumatic.—A device for raising sewage, sludge, or other liquid by alternately admitting such through an inward swinging check valve into the bottom of an airtight pot and then discharging it through an outward swinging check valve by admitting compressed air to the pot above the liquid.

Elutriation.—A process of sludge conditioning in which certain constituents are removed by successive decantations with fresh water or plant effluent, thereby reducing the demand for conditioning chemicals.

F

Factor.—Frequently a ratio used to express operating conditions.

    Load.—The ratio of the average load carried by any operation to the maximum load carried, during a given period of time, expressed as a percentage. The load may consist of almost anything, such as electrical power, number of persons served, amount of water carried by a conduit, etc.

    Power.—An electrical term describing the ratio of the true power passing through an electric circuit to the product of the volts times the amperes in the circuit. It is a measure of the lag or lead of the current in respect to the voltage. While the power of a current is the product of the voltage times the amperes in the circuit, in alternating current the voltage and amperes are not always in phase, hence the true power may be less than that determined by the product of volts times amperes.

Filter.—A term meaning (1) an oxidizing bed (2) a device for removing solids from a liquid by some type of strainer.

    Biological.—A bed of sand, gravel, broken stone, or other media through which sewage flows or trickles, which depends on biological action for its effectiveness.

    High-Rate.—A trickling filter operated at a high average daily dosing rate usually between 10-30 mgd per acre, sometimes including recirculation of effluent.

    Low-Rate.—A trickling filter designed to receive a small load of BOD per unit volume of filtering material and to have a low dosage rate per unit of surface area (usually 1 to 4 mgd per acre). Also called Standard Rate Filter.

    Roughing.—A sewage filter of relatively coarse material operated at a high rate as a preliminary treatment.

    Sand.—A filter in which sand is used as a filtering medium.

    Sand Sludge.—A bed of sand used to dewater sludge by drainage and evaporation.

    Sludge.—The solid matter in sewage that is removed by settling in primary and secondary settling tanks.

    Trickling.—A treatment unit consisting of a material such as broken stone, clinkers, slate, slats, or brush, over which sewage is distributed and applied in drops, films, or spray, from troughs, drippers, moving distributors, or fixed nozzles, and through which it trickles to the underdrains, giving opportunity for the formation of zoological slimes which clarify and oxidize the sewage.

    Vacuum.—A filter consisting of a cylindrical drum mounted on a horizontal axis, covered with filtering material made of wool, felt, cotton, saran, nylon, dacron, polyethylene or similar substance, by stainless steel coil springs or metal screen, revolving with a partial submergence in the liquid. A vacuum is maintained under the cloth for the larger part of a revolution to extract moisture. The cake is scraped off continuously.

Filtrate.—The effluent of a Filter.

Floc.—Small gelatinous masses, formed in a liquid by the addition of coagulants thereto or through biochemical processes or by agglomeration.

Flocculator.—An apparatus for the formation of floc in water or sewage.

Flotation.—A method of raising suspended matter to the surface of the liquid in a tank as scum—by aeration, by the evolution of gas, chemicals, electrolysis, heat, or bacterial decomposition—and the subsequent removal of the scum by skimming.

Freeboard.—The vertical distance between the normal maximum level of the surface of the liquid in a conduit, reservoir, tank, canal, etc., and the top of the sides of an open conduit, the top of a dam or levee, etc., which is provided so that waves and other movements of the liquid will not overtop the confining structure.

Fungi.—Small nonchlorophyll-bearing plants which lack roots, stems, or leaves and which occur (among other places) in water, sewage, or sewage effluents, growing best in the absence of light. Their decomposition after death may cause disagreeable tastes and odors in water; in some sewage treatment processes they are helpful and in others they are detrimental.

G

Gage.—A device for measuring any physical magnitude.
    Float.—A device for measuring the elevation of the surface of a liquid, the actuation element being a buoyant float which rests upon the surface of the liquid.
    Indicator.—A gage that shows by means of an index, pointer, dial, etc., the instantaneous value of such characteristics as depth, pressure, velocity, stage, discharge, or the movements or positions of water-controlling devices.
    Mercury.—A gage wherein pressure of a fluid is measured by the height of a column of mercury which the fluid pressure will sustain. The mercury is usually contained in a tube, attached to the vessel or pipe containing the fluid.
    Pressure.—A device for registering the pressure of solids, liquids, or gases. It may be graduated to the register pressure in any units desired.

Garbage, Ground.—Garbage shredded or ground by apparatus installed in sinks and discharged to the sewerage system; or garbage collected and hauled to a central grinding station, shredded preliminary to disposal, usually, by digestion with sewage sludge.

Gas.—One of the three states of matter.
    Sewage.—(1) The gas produced by the septicization of sewage. (2) The gas produced during the digestion of sewage sludge, usually collected and utilized.
    Sewer.—Gas evolved in sewers from the decomposition of the organic matter in the sewage. Also any gas present in the sewerage system, even though it is from gas mains, gasoline, cleaning fluid, etc.

Gasification.—The transformation of sewage solids into gas in the decomposition of sewage.

Go Devil.—A scraper with self-adjusting spring blades, inserted in a pipe line, and carried forward by the fluid pressure for clearing away accumulations, tuberculations, etc.

Grade.—(1) The inclination or slope of a stream channel, conduit, or natural ground surface, usually expressed in terms of the ratio or percentage of number of units of vertical rise or fall per unit of horizontal distance. (2) The elevation of the invert of the bottom of a pipe line, canal, culvert, sewer, etc. (3) The finished surface of a canal bed, road bed, top of an embankment. or bottom of an excavation. (4) In plumbing, the fall in inches per foot of length of pipe.

Grease.—In sewage, grease including fats, waxes, free fatty acids, calcium and magnesium soaps, mineral oils, and other non-fatty materials. The type of solvent used for its extraction should be stated.

Grinder, Screenings.—A device for grinding, shredding, or comminuting material removed from sewage by screens.

Grit.—The heavy mineral matter in water or sewage, such as gravel, cinders, etc.

H

Head.—Energy per unit weight of liquid at a specified point. It is expressed in feet.

    Dynamic.—The head against which a pump works.

    Friction.—The head lost by water flowing in a stream or conduit as the result of the disturbances set up by the contact between the moving water and its containing conduit, and by intermolecular friction. In laminar flow the head lost is approximately proportional to the first power of the velocity; in turbulent flow to a higher power, approximately the square of the velocity. While strictly speaking, head losses due to bends, expansions, obstructions, impact, etc., are not included in this term, the usual practice is to include all such head losses under this term.

    Loss of.—The decrease in head between two points.

    Static.—The vertical distance between the free level of the source of supply, and the point of free discharge, or the level of the free surface.

    Total Dynamic.—The difference between the elevation corresponding to the pressure at the discharge flange of a pump and the elevation corresponding to the vacuum or pressure at the suction flange of the pump, corrected to the same datum plane, plus the velocity head at the discharge flange of the pump, minus the velocity head at the suction flange of the pump. It includes the friction head.

    Velocity.—The theoretical vertical height through which a liquid body may be raised due to its kinetic energy. It is equal to the square of the velocity divided by twice the acceleration due to gravity.

Humus.—The dark or black carboniferous residue in the soil resulting from the decomposition of vegetable tissues of plants originally growing therein. Residues similar in appearance and behavior are found in well-digested sludges and in activated sludge.

Hypochlorite.—Compounds of chlorine in which the radical (OC1) is present. They are usually inorganic.

    High Test.—A solid triple salt containing Ca (OC1) 2 to the extent that the fresh solid has approximately 70 percent available chlorine. It is not the same as chlorinated lime.

    Sodium.—A solution containing NaOC1, prepared by passing chlorine into solutions of soda ash, or reacting soda ash solutions with high-test hypochlorites and decanting from the precipitated sludge.

I

Imhoff Cone.—A conically shaped graduated glass vessel used to measure approximately the volume of settleable solids in various liquids of sewage origin.

Imhoff Tank.—See Tank, Imhoff

Impeller.—The rotating part of a centrifugal pump, containing the curved vanes.

    Closed.—An impeller having the side walls extended from the outer circumference of the suction opening to the vane tips.

    Nonclogging.—An impeller of the open, closed, or semi-closed type designed with large passages for passing large solids.

Open.—An impeller without attached side walls.

Screw.—The helical impeller of a screw pump.

Index, Sludge Volume.—The volume is milliliters occupied by one gram of dry solids after the aerated mixed liquor settles 30 minutes, commonly referred to as the Mohlman index.

Influent.—Sewage, water, or other liquid, raw or partly treated, flowing into a reservoir, basin, or treatment plant, or part thereof.

L

Lagoon, Sludge.—A relatively shallow basin, or natural depression, used for the storage or digestion of sludge, and sometimes for its ultimate detention or dewatering.

Lift, Air.—A device for raising liquid by injecting air in and near the bottom of a riser pipe submerged in the liquid to be raised.

Liquefaction.—The changing of the organic matter in sewage from an insoluble to a soluble state, and effecting a reduction in its solid contents.

Liquor.—Any liquid.

Mixed.—A mixture of activated sludge and sewage in the aeration tank undergoing activated sludge treatment.

Supernatant. — (1) The liquor overlying deposited solids. (2) The liquid in a sludge-digestion tank which lies between the sludge at the bottom and the floating scum at the top.

Loading.—The time rate at which material is applied to a treatment device involving length, area, or volume or other design factor.

BOD, Filter.—The pounds of oxygen demand in the applied liquid per unit of filter bed area, or volume of stone per day.

Weir.—Gallons overflow per day per foot of weir length.

M

Main, Force.—A pipe line on the discharge side of a water or sewage pumping station, usually under pressure.

Manometer.—An instrument for measuring pressure; usually it consists of a U-shaped tube containing a liquid, the surface of which in one end of the tube moves proportionally with changes in pressure upon the liquid in the other end. The term is also applied to a tube type of differential pressure gage.

Matter.—Solids, liquids, and gases.

Inorganic.—Chemical substances of mineral origin. They are not usually volatile with heat.

Organic.—Chemical substances of animal, vegetable and industrial origin. They include most carbon compounds, combustible and volatile with heat.

Suspended.—(1) Solids in suspension in sewage or effluent. (2) Commonly used for solids in suspension in sewage or effluent which can readily be removed by filtering in a laboratory.

Microorganism.—Minute organisms either plant or animal, invisible or barely visible to the naked eye.

Moisture, Percentage.—The water content of sludge expressed as the ratio of the loss in weight after drying at 103°C, to the original weight of the sample, multiplied by one hundred.

Mold.—See Fungi.

Most Probable Number, (MPN).—In the testing of bacterial density by the dilution method, that number of organisms per unit volume which, in accordance with statistical theory, would be more likely than any other possible number to yield the observed test result or which would yield the observed test result with the greatest frequency. Expressed as density of organisms per 100 ml.

N

Nitrification.—The oxidation of ammonia nitrogen into nitrates through biochemical action.

O

Overflow Rate.—One of the criteria for the design of settling tanks in treatment plants; expressed in gallons per day per square foot of surface area in the settling tank. See Surface Settling Rate.

Oxidation.—The addition of oxygen, removal of hydrogen, or the increase in the valence of an element.

    Biochemical.—See Oxidation, Sewage.

    Biological.—See Oxidation, Sewage.

    Direct.—Oxidation of substances in sewage without the benefit of living organisms, by the direct application of air or oxidizing agents such as chlorine.

    Sewage.—The process whereby, through the agency of living organisms in the presence of oxygen, the organic matter contained in sewage is converted into a more stable form.

Oxygen.—A chemical element.

    Available.—The quantity of uncombined or free oxygen dissolved in the water of a stream.

    Balance.—The relation between the biochemical oxygen demand of a sewage or treatment plant effluent and the oxygen available in the diluting water.

    Consumed.—The quantity of oxygen taken from potassium permanganate in solution by a liquid containing organic matter. Commonly regarded as an index of the carbonaceous matter present. Time and temperature must be specified. The chemical oxygen demand (COD) uses potassium dichromate.

    Deficiency.—The additional quantity of oxygen required to satisfy the biochemical oxygen demand in a given liquid. Usually expressed in parts per million.

    Dissolved.—Usually designated as DO. The oxygen dissolved in sewage, water or other liquid usually expressed in parts per million or percent of saturation.

    Residual.—The dissolved oxygen content of a stream after deoxygenation has begun.

    Sag.—A curve that represents the profile of dissolved oxygen content along the course of a stream, resulting from deoxygenation associated with biochemical oxidation of organic matter, and reoxygenation through the absorption of atmospheric oxygen and through biological photosynthesis.

P

Parts Per Million.—Milligrams per liter expressing the concentration of a specified component in a dilute sewage. A ratio of pounds per million pounds, grams per million grams, etc.

Percolation.—The flow or trickling of a liquid downward through a contact or filtering medium. The liquid may or may not fill the pores of the medium.

Period.—A time interval.

Aeration.—(1) The theoretical time, usually expressed in hours that the mixed liquor is subjected to aeration in an aeration tank undergoing activated sludge treatment; is equal to (a) the volume of the tank divided by (b) the volumetric rate of flow of the sewage and return sludge. (2) The theoretical time that water is subjected to aeration.

Detention.—The theoretical time required to displace the contents of a tank or unit at a given rate of discharge (volume divided by rate of discharge).

Flowing-Through.—The average time required for a small unit volume of liquid to pass through a basin from inlet to outlet. In a tank where there is no short-circuiting, and no spaces, the detention period and the flowing-through period are the same.

pH.—The logarithm of the reciprocal of the hydrogen-ion concentration. It is not the same as the alkalinity and cannot be calculated therefrom.

Plankton.—Drifting organisms, usually microscopic.

Pollution.—The addition of sewage, industrial wastes, or other harmful or objectionable material to water.

Ponding, Filter.—See Pooling, Filter.

Pooling, Filter.—The formation of pools of sewage on the surface of filters caused by clogging.

Population Equivalent.—(1) The calculated population which would normally contribute the same amount of biochemical oxygen demand (BOD) per day. A common base is 0.167 lb. of 5-day BOD per capita per day. (2) For an industrial waste, the estimated number of people contributing sewage equal in strength to a unit volume of the waste or to some other unit involved in producing or manufacturing a particular commodity.

Pre-Aeration.—A preparatory treatment of sewage comprising aeration to remove gases, add oxygen, or promote flotation of grease, and aid coagulation.

Precipitation, Chemical.—Precipitation induced by addition of chemicals.

Pressure.—Pounds per square inch or square foot.

Atmospheric.—The pressure exerted by the atmosphere at any point. Such pressure decreases the elevation of the point above sea level increases. One atmosphere is equal to 14.7 lb. per sq. in., 29.92 in. or 760 mm of mercury column or 33.90 ft. of water column at average sea level under standard conditions.

Hydrostatic.—The pressure, expressed as a total force per unit of area, exerted by a body of water at rest.

Negative.—A pressure less than the local atmospheric pressure at a given point.

Process.—A sequence of operations.

Activated Sludge.—A biological sewage treatment process in which a mixture of sewage and activated sludge is agitated and aerated. The activated sludge is subsequently separated from the treated sewage (mixed liquor) by sedimentation, and wasted or returned to the process as needed. The treated sewage overflows the weir of the settling tank in which separation from the sludge takes place.

Biological.—The process by which the life activities of bacteria, and other microorganisms in the search for food, break down complex organic materials into simple, more stable substances. Self-purification of sewage-polluted streams, sludge digestion, and all so-called secondary sewage treatments result from this process. Also called Biochemical Process.

Pump.—A device used to increase the head on a liquid.

Booster.—A pump installed on a pipe line to raise the pressure of the water on the discharge side of the pump.

Centrifugal, Fluid.—A pump consisting of an impeller fixed on a rotating shaft and enclosed in a casing, having an inlet and a discharge connection. The rotating impeller creates pressure in the liquid by the velocity derived from centrifugal force.

Centrifugal, Screw.—A centrifugal pump having a screw-type impeller; may be axial-flow, or combined axial and radial-flow, type.

Centrifugal, Closed.—A centrifugal pump where the impeller is built with the vanes enclosed within circular disks.

Diaphragm.—A pump in which a flexible diaphragm, generally of rubber, is the operating part; it is fastened at the outer rim; when the diaphragm is moved in one direction, suction is exerted and when it is moved in the opposite direction, the liquid is forced through a discharge valve.

Double-Suction.—A centrifugal pump with suction pipes connected to the casing from both sides.

Duplex.—A reciprocating pump consisting of two cylinders placed side by side and connected to the same suction and discharge pipe, the pistons moving so that one exerts suction while the other exerts pressure, with the result that the discharge from the pump is continuous.

Horizontal Screw.—A pump with a horizontal cylindrical casing, in which operates a runner with radial blades, like those of a ship's propeller. The pump has a high efficiency at low heads and high discharges, and is used extensively in drainage work.

Mixed Flow.—A centrifugal pump in which the head is developed partly by centrifugal force and partly by the lift of the vanes on the liquid.

Open Centrifugal.—A centrifugal pump where the impeller is built with a set of independent vanes.

Propeller.—A centrifugal pump which develops most of its head by the propelling or lifting action of the vanes on the liquids.

Purification.—The removal, by natural or artificial methods, or objectionable matter from water.

Putrefaction.—Biological decomposition of organic matter with the production of ill-smelling products associated with anaerobic conditions.

Putrescibility. — (1) The relative tendency of organic matter to undergo decomposition in the absence of oxygen. (2) The susceptibility of waste waters, sewage, effluent, or sludge to putrefaction. (3) Term used in water or sewage analysis to define stability of a polluted water or raw or partially treated sewage.

Q

Quicklime.—A calcined material, the major part of which is calcium oxide or calcium oxide in natural association with a lesser amount of magnesium oxide, capable of slaking with water.

R

Rack.—An arrangement of parallel bars.

Bar.—A screen composed of parallel bars, either vertical or inclined, placed in a waterway to catch floating debris, and from which the screenings may be raked. Also called rack.

Coarse.—A rack with 3/4 inch to 6 inch spaces between bars.

Fine.—Generally used for a screen or rack which has openings of 3/32 to 3/16 inches. Some screens have less than 3/32 inch openings.

Radius, Hydraulic.—The cross-sectional area of a stream of water divided by the length of that part of its periphery in contact with its containing conduit; the ratio of area to wetted perimeter.

Rate.—The result of dividing one concrete number by another.

Filtration.—The rate of application of water or sewage to a filter, usually expressed in million gallons per acre per day, or gallons per minute per square foot.

Infiltration.—The rate, usually expressed in cubic feet per second, or million gallons per day per mile of waterway, at which ground water enters an infiltration ditch or gallery, drain, sewer, or other underground conduit.

Surface Settling.—Gallons per day per square foot of free horizontal water surface. Used in design of sedimentation tanks.

Reaeration.—The absorption of oxygen by a liquid, the dissolved oxygen content of which has been depleted.

Reaeration, Sludge.—The continuous aeration of sludge after its initial aeration in the activated sludge process.

Recirculation. — (1) The refiltration of all or a portion of the effluent in a high-rate trickling filter for the purpose of maintaining a uniform high rate through the filter. (2) The return of effluent to the incoming flow to reduce its strength.

Reduction.—The decrease in a specific variable.

    Over-All.—The percentage reduction in the final effluent as compared to the raw sewage.

    Percentage.—The ratio of material removed from water or sewage by treatment, to the material originally present (expressed as a percentage).

    Sludge.—The reduction in the quantity and change in character of sewage sludge as the result of digestion.

Regulator.—A device or apparatus for controlling the quantity of sewage admitted to an intercepting sewer or a unit of a sewage treatment plant.

Reoxygenation.—The replenishment of oxygen in a stream from (1) dilution water entering stream, (2) biological reoxygenation through the activities of certain oxygen-producing plants, and (3) atmospheric reaction.

Residual, Chlorine.—See Chlorine, residual.

Rotor.—The member of an electric generator or water wheel which rotates.

S

Screen.—A device with openings, generally of uniform size, used to retain or remove suspended or floating solids in flowing water or sewage, and to prevent them from entering an intake or passing a given point in a conduit. The screening element may consist of parallel bars, rods, wires, grating, wire mesh, or perforated plate, and the openings may be of any shape, although they are generally circular or rectangular. The device may also be used to segregate granular material, such as sand, crushed rock, and soil, into various sizes.

Scum.—A mass of sewage matter which floats on the surface of sewage.

Second-Foot.—An abbreviated expression for cubic foot per second.

Sedimentation.—The process of subsidence and deposition of suspended matter carried by water, sewage, or other liquids, by gravity. It is usually accomplished by reducing the velocity of the liquid below the point where it can transport the suspended material. Also called Settling. See Precipitation, Chemical.

    Final.—Settling of partly settled, flocculated or oxidized sewage in a final tank.

    Plain.—The sedimentation of suspended matter in a liquid unaided by chemicals or other special means, and without provision for the decomposition of deposited solids in contact with the sewage.

Seeding, Sludge.—The inoculation of undigested sewage solids with sludge that has undergone decomposition, for the purpose of introducing favorable organisms, thereby accelerating the initial stages of digestion.

Self-Purification.—The natural processes of purification in a moving or still body of water whereby the bacterial content is reduced, the BOD is largely satisfied, the organic content is stabilized, and the dissolved oxygen returned to normal.

Sewage.—Largely the water supply of a community after it has been fouled by various uses. From the standpoint of source it may be a combination of the liquid or water-carried wastes from residences, business buildings, and institutions, together with those from industrial establishments, and with such ground water, surface water, and storm water as may be present.

    Domestic.—Sewage derived principally from dwellings, business buildings, institutions, and the like. (It may or may not contain ground water, surface water, or storm water.)

    Fresh.—Sewage of recent origin containing dissolved oxygen at the point of examination.

    Industrial.—Sewage in which industrial wastes predominate.

    Stable.—Sewage in which the organic matter has been stabilized.

    Raw.—Sewage prior to receiving any treatment.

    Sanitary.—(1) Domestic sewage with storm and surface water excluded. (2) Sewage discharging from the sanitary conveniences of dwellings (including apartment houses and hotels), office buildings, factories, or institutions. (3) The water supply of a community after it has been used and discharged into a sewer.

    Septic.—Sewage undergoing putrefaction under anaerobic conditions.

    Settled.—Sewage from which most of the settleable solids have been removed by sedimentation.

    Stale.—A sewage containing little or no oxygen, but as yet free from putrefaction.

Sewer.—A pipe or conduit, generally closed, but normally not flowing full, for carrying sewage and other waste liquids.

    Branch.—A sewer which receives sewage from a relatively small area, and discharges into a main sewer.

    Combined.—A sewer receiving both surface runoff and sewage.

    House.—A pipe conveying sewage from a single building to a common sewer or point of immediate disposal.

    Intercepting.—A sewer which receives dry-weather flow from a number of transverse sewers or outlets and frequently additional predetermined quantities of storm water (if from a combined system), and conducts such waters to a point for treatment or disposal.

    Lateral.—A sewer which discharges into a branch or other sewer and has no other common sewer tributary to it.

    Main. — (1) A sewer to which one or more branch sewers are tributary. Also called Trunk Sewer. (2) In plumbing, the public sewer in a street, alley, or other premises under the jurisdiction of a municipality.

    Sanitary.—A sewer which carries sewage and to which storm, surface, and ground waters are not intentionally admitted.

    Separate.—See Sewer, Sanitary.

    Storm.—A sewer which carries storm water and surface water, street wash and other wash waters, or drainage, but excludes sewage and industrial wastes. Also called Storm Drain.

    Trunk—A sewer which receives many tributary branches and serves a large territory. See Sewer, Main.

    Outfall.—A sewer which receives the sewage from a collecting system and carries it to a point of final discharge.

Outlet.—The point of final discharge of sewage or treatment plant effluent.
Sewerage.—A comprehensive term which includes facilities for collecting, pumping, treating, and disposing of sewage; the sewerage system and the sewage treatment works.
Shredder.—A device for size reduction.
    Screenings.—A device which disintegrates screenings.
    Sludge.—An apparatus to break down lumps in air-dried digested sludge.
Siphon.—A closed conduit, a portion of which lies above the hydraulic grade line. This results in a pressure less than atmospheric in that portion, and hence requires that a vacuum be created to start flow.
Skimmer, Grease.—A device for removing floating grease or scum from the surface of sewage in a tank.
Skimming.—The process of removing floating grease or scum from the surface of sewage in a tank.
Sleek.—The thin oily film usually present which gives characteristic appearance to the surface of water into which sewage or oily waste has discharged. Also termed slick.
Sloughing.—The phenomenon associated with trickling filters and contact aerators. whereby slime and solids accumulated in the media are discharged with the effluent.
Sludge.—The accumulated settled solids deposited from sewage or industrial wastes, raw or treated. in tanks or basins, and containing more or less water to form a semiliquid mass.
    Activated.—Sludge floc produced in raw or settled sewage by the growth of zoogleal bacteria and other organisms in the presence of dissolved oxygen, and accumulated in sufficient concentration by returning floc previously formed.
    Bulking.—A phenomenon that occurs in activated sludge plants whereby the sludge occupies excessive volumes and will not concentrate readily.
    Conditioning.—Treatment of liquid sludge preliminary to dewatering and drainability, usually by the addition of chemicals.
    Dewatering.—The process of removing a part of the water in sludge by any method, such as draining, evaporation, pressing, centrifuging, exhausting, passing between rollers, or acid flotation, with or without heat. It involves reducing from a liquid to a spadable condition rather than merely changing the density of the liquid (concentration) on the one hand or drying (as in a kiln) on the other.
    Digestion.—The process by which organic or volatile matter in sludge is gasified, liquefied, mineralized. or converted into more stable organic matter, through the activities of living organisms.
    Humus.—See **Humus**.
Solids.—Material in the solid state.
    Dissolved.—Solids which are present in solution.
    Nonsettleable.—Finely divided suspended solids which will not subside in quiescent water, sewage, or other liquid in a reasonable period. Such period is commonly, though arbitrarily, taken as two hours.
    Settleable.—Suspended solids which will subside in quiescent water, sewage, or other liquid in a reasonable period. Such period is commonly, though arbitrarily, taken as one hour. Also called Settling Solids.
    Suspended.—The quantity of material deposited when a quantity of water, sewage, or other liquid is filtered through an asbestos mat in a Gooch crucible.
    Total.—The solids in water, sewage, or other liquids; it includes the suspended solids (largely removable by filter paper) and the filterable solids (those which pass through filter paper).

Volatile.—The quantity of solids in water, sewage, or other liquid, lost on ignition of the total solids.

Squeegee.—(1) A device, generally with a soft rubber edge, used for dislodging and removing deposited sewage solids from the walls and bottoms of sedimentation tanks. (2) The metal blades attached to the lower arms of a clarifier mechanism to move the sludge along the tank bottom.

Stability.—The ability of any substance, such as sewage, effluent, or digested sludge, to resist putrefaction. It is the antonym of putrescibility.

Standard Methods.—Methods of analysis of water, sewage, and sludge approved by a Joint Committee of the American Public Health Association. American Water Works Association, and Federation of Sewage Works Associations.

Stator.—The stationary member of an electric generator or motor.

Sterilization.—The destruction of all living organisms, ordinarily through the agency of heat or of some chemical.

T

Tank.—A circular or rectangular vessel.

    Detritus.—A detention chamber larger than a grit chamber, usually with provision for removing the sediment without interrupting the flow of sewage. A settling tank of short detention period designed, primarily, to remove heavy settleable solids.

    Final Settling.—A tank through which the effluent from a trickling filter, or aeration or contact aeration tank flows for the purpose of removing the settleable solids.

    Flocculating.—A tank used for the formation of floc by the agitation of liquids.

    Imhoff.—A deep two-storied sewage tank originally patented by Karl Imhoff. consisting of an upper or continuous flow sedimentation chamber and a lower or sludge-digestion chamber. The floor of the upper chamber slopes steeply to trapped slots, through which solids may slide into the lower chamber. The lower chamber receives no fresh sewage directly, but is provided with gas vents and with means for drawing digested sludge from near the bottom.

    Primary Settling.—The first settling tank through which sewage is passed in a treatment works.

    Secondary.—A tank following a trickling filter or activated sludge aeration chamber.

    Sedimentation.—A tank or basin. in which water, sewage, or other liquid containing settleable solids, is retained for a sufficient time, and in which the velocity of flow is sufficiently low, to remove by gravity a part of the suspended matter. Usually, in sewage treatment, the detention period is short enough to avoid anaerobic decomposition. Also termed Settling or Subsidence Tank.

    Septic.—A single-story settling tank in which the settled sludge is in immediate contact with the sewage flowing through the tank, while the organic solids are decomposed by anaerobic bacterial action.

    Sludge-Digestion--See Digester.

Thickener, Sludge.—A type of sedimentation tank in which the sludge is permitted to settle, usually equipped with scrapers traveling along the bottom of the tank which push the settled sludge to a sump, from which it is removed by gravity or by pumping.

Treatment.—Any definite process for modifying the state of matter.

    Preliminary.—The conditioning of an industrial waste at its source prior 'to discharge, to remove or to neutralize substances injurious to sewers and treatment processes or to effect a partial reduction in load on the treatment process. In the treatment process, unit operations which prepare the liquor for subsequent major operations.

Primary.—The first major (sometimes the only) treatment in a sewage treatment works, usually sedimentation. The removal of a high percentage of suspended matter but little or no colloidal and dissolved matter.

Secondary.—The treatment of sewage by biological methods after primary treatment by sedimentation.

Sewage.—Any artificial process to which sewage is subjected in order to remove or alter its objectional constituents and thus to render it less offensive or dangerous.

Trap, Flame.—A device containing a fine metal gauze placed in a gas pipe, which prevents a flame from traveling back in the pipe and causing an explosion. See Arrester, Flame.

V

Venturi Meter.—A meter for measuring flow of water or other fluid through closed conduits or pipes, consisting of a Venturi tube and one of several proprietary forms of flow registering devices. The device was developed as a measuring device and patented by Clemens Herschel.

W

Waste Stabilization Pond.—Any pond, natural or artificial, receiving raw or partially treated sewage or waste, in which stabilization occurs due to sunlight, air, and microorganisms.

Water, Potable.—Water which does not contain objectionable pollution, contamination, minerals, or infection, and is considered satisfactory for domestic consumption.

Weir.—A dam with an edge or notch, sometimes arranged for measuring liquid flow.

    Effluent—A weir at the outflow end of a sedimentation basin or other hydraulic structure.

    Influent—A weir at the inflow end of a sedimentation basin.

    Rectangular.—A weir whose notch is rectangular in shape.

    Triangular.—A weir whose notch is triangular in shape, usually used to measure very small flows. Also called a V-notch.

    Peripheral.—The outlet weir in a circular settling tank, extending around the inside of its circumference and over which the effluent discharges.

    Rate.—See Loading, Weir.

Z

Zooglea.—A jelly-like matrix developed by bacteria, associated with growths in oxidizing beds.